THE INCIDENT
AT MASSENA

Also by the author:
No Haven for the Oppressed
Pogromchik

THE INCIDENT AT MASSENA

The Blood Libel in America

SAUL S. FRIEDMAN

STEIN AND DAY/*Publishers*/New York

Library of Congress Cataloging in Publication Data

Friedman, Saul S., 1937–
    The incident at Massena.

    1. Blood accusation.   2.   Jews in Massena, N. Y.—
History.   3.   Massena, N. Y.—History.   I.   Title.
BM585.2.F74   296.3   78-6406
ISBN 0-8128-2526-8

For
my mother, Rebecca Friedman;
my brother, Norman;
and my son, Jason
three generations
of love, wisdom, and joy

PREFACE

*T*he basic tools of an historian are his sources—his proofs—his notes. It was as a result of poring over the end notes to Joshua Trachtenberg's essay on persecution, *The Devil and the Jews: The Medieval Conception of the Jew and Its Relation to Modern Antisemitism,* in 1962 that I first found reference to the incident at Massena. It was not until 1971, however, that I was able to pursue the matter with a trip to the little town on the Saint Lawrence River. This was followed by visits to Syracuse, Rome (New York), Albany, New York City, Pittsburgh, Cleveland, and Cincinnati in an effort to reconstruct what actually transpired in Massena in September 1928.

Generally, I found people everywhere cooperative and willing to talk. Among the Jewish community in Massena, I was especially aided by Dora Cohen and Mimi Klein, daughters of Jake Shulkin; Abe Kauffman, son of the town's "first" Jewish inhabitant; Jack Jacobs and Lou Greenblatt, unofficial historians of the Adath Israel Congregation; Saul and Jeanette Rosenbaum, two old-timers who went through those difficult days as adults; and, whether she appreciated the fact or not, Minnie Slavin, with whom I spent a lovely afternoon discussing Jewish life in the North Country.

Massena's Gentiles were also most helpful. My thanks go out to Marie Elden-Brown, town historian; Cole Cummins, at ninety-three still the town intellectual; attorney Seward Hanmer; the late Leonard Prince, editor of the *Massena Observer;* his successor Pat McKeon and her assistant John Maines who agreed that the story must be told; Ernest Wagar, onetime secretary of the Chamber of Commerce; Dale Wright, chief of police; Dave and Marion Griffiths; Anna and Margaret Pilialoglous, Ella Lahey and Eleanor Dumas, Sam Cappione, George Ure, Emily Bushnell, Captain Harry Hollander, and Joseph Burke.

In Rome, New York, I spent much time with Ben Shulkin, another of Jake Shulkin's children. In Syracuse, my source was the wonderfully alert octogenarian, Eli Friedman, who was then recuperating from an operation at Syracuse Community General Hospital. In New York City, I was aided by Boris Smolar of the Jewish Telegraph Agency; Samuel Brennglass, son of Rabbi Berel Brennglass; and assistant librarians at the American Jewish Committee and American Jewish Congress. Additional information came from the Wise Records of the American Jewish Historical Society at Brandeis University; the Alfred E. Smith Papers, Museum of the City of New York; and the Smith Papers, State Education Library, Albany, New York. In Albany, my searches were made less painful by Bob Boberman and Dr. Lewis Tocker of the State Records Center; Al Singer of the State Legal Department; and Superinten-

dent William Kirwan and Officers Bardosi and Vain-
auskaus of the State Highway Patrol. And in Rochester,
my thanks to a gracious lady, Mrs. William Shulkin.

In the process of reconstructing the events of that fall,
I have been hampered by confused and conflicting stories, a dearth of written records, and the temporary
obstinacy of one archivist to part with documents. I
have found newspapers, especially the New York press,
to be generally unreliable. Some written reports, moreover, are at great divergence with one another, and
much oral testimony is equally confused. Some sources
flatly admit they cannot distinguish between what they
actually recall and what they think they *should* recall.

Because of problems posed by oral history, several
alternatives have been suggested to me by well-meaning
friends. One was to render the account in fictional form,
along lines recently attempted by Richard Kluger in his
Members of the Tribe, which deals with the Leo Frank
Affair. Such a procedure, I have been assured, would
guarantee not only a "best-seller," but also a movie
contract. Tempting as that may be, the skills of an
historian are not the same as those of a novelist. Perhaps one day a Michener or Malamud will come along
with such a work.

Others have suggested that I emulate the fashion of
Thucydides, who wrote 2,300 years ago:

> I have found it difficult to remember the precise
> words used in the speeches which I listened to myself
> and my various informants have experienced the
> same difficulty; so my method has been, while keep-
> ing as closely as possible to the general sense of the
> words that were actually used, to make the speakers
> say, what, in my opinion, was called for by each
> situation.

Preface

I have also rejected this course as unwise. To tamper with events as they unfolded in September and October 1928 would be to compromise the reality of what happened. I do not want people saying that "that could never happen in America" or that this is a script for a "Movie of the Week." What is described on these pages did happen in an America that prides itself on ethnic diversity and toleration. I have taken great pains to document every statement. Where I have digressed into conjecture, I have so advised the reader.

In writing this book, it has not been my intention to rekindle the faggots of hatred in Massena or any other town. I have pledged to those with whom I spoke that such research would not embarrass them. Because of the historic importance of the blood libel, however, and because I want people to know the facts, I deliberately did not alter the names of any of the principals in the affair. I affirm that this book has been written not from vindictiveness but with a view toward educating Jew and Gentile alike on the baseness of the ritual murder canard so that what happened at Massena might never happen again.

Finally, my appreciation to my assistants Mark Connelly, Mike Billirakis, Skevos Corfias, and Susan Fogaras, who helped with technical aspects of the manuscript; to Youngstown State University for extending two graduate research grants and a university research professorship for completion of this project; and to my wife, Nancy, who has been my rock during the good days and the bad.

Youngstown, Ohio
Winter 1978

THE INCIDENT
AT MASSENA

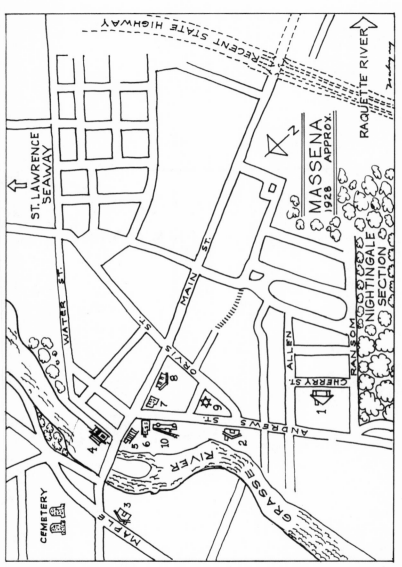

1. Griffiths Residence, Cherry Street 2. Hawes Residence, Andrews Street 3. Shulkin Residence, Maple Street
4. Shulkin and Slavin's Store, Water Street 5. Stone and Co., Main Street 6. Comnas' Crystal Palace in Central
Building 7. White's Hotel 8. Massena City Hall 9. Adath Israel Synagogue 10. Massena Fire Station

1

For most Americans, the fall of 1928 was a happy, exciting time. The ever-upward march of the bullish stock market seemed to confirm millionaire John Raskob's instruction that "everyone ought to be rich." For once, the begrimed steelworker in Steubenville and the dried-out dowager in Shaker Heights shared a common concern—the price of RCA or Montgomery Ward. Tiffany's dangled before the readers of a prominent magazine a diamond bauble valued at $100,000. The permanently impoverished runner in Manhattan's garment jungle fantasized that glory would be his when his beloved Yankees met and defeated the St. Louis Cardinals in the World Series. Methodist farmers in Willshire, Ohio, who had never seen a dirigible, marveled when they read in the Fort Wayne papers of the *Graf Zeppelin,* which had completed a 620-mile cruise, averaging 80 miles per hour, while its crew served up gourmet meals to its passengers. A confident, euphoric America wondered what limits there might be to man's achievements when its athletes swept the summer Olympic Games at Amsterdam, when its writers contributed *Strange Interlude* and *The Bridge of San Luis Rey,* when science could now deliver Al Jolson or Mickey Mouse in Vitaphone and promise through the tinkerings of J. L. Baird the synchronization of television and radio in the near future. The nation's engineering feats—the Holland Tunnel connecting New Jersey and Manhattan; the 750-foot cantilever Outerbridge Crossing from Perth Amboy, New Jersey, to Staten Island; and the series of Babellike towers including the 77-story Chrysler Building, the 90-story Bank of Manhattan Building, and the 102-story Empire State Building—all testified to man's proximity to the messianic era.

There was something for everyone in this fabulous age. Nature supplied enough signs to vindicate perpetual cynics in their Jeremiads about society's impending collapse. On March 13, the Saint Francis Water Supply Dam 40 miles north of Los Angeles collapsed, killing 450 people and destroying 700 houses. Two months later, 195 men perished at Mather, Pennsylvania, in the worst mining disaster in more than a decade. That summer, the wreck of an IRT train under Times Square left another 18 dead and 97 injured. While farmers from Arkansas to the Dakotas reckoned with a continuing drought that would make the Plains into a Dust Bowl in but a few years, the Lake Okeechobee region near West Palm Beach, Florida, was ravaged by hurricane between September 12 and 17. At least 4,000 persons died in the worst American storm tragedy since the Galveston Flood of 1900.

Equally depressing news could be found elsewhere around the world: the crash of the dirigible *Italia* in the Arctic on May 25, with 7 crewmen lost; the sinking of the Chilean ship *Angames* in Araunco Bay on July 7, with 291 casualties; and the eruption of Mount Etna, wiping out the town of Mascati, Sicily, and wreaking destruction estimated at $10,000,000. There was civil war in China, plague in the Congo, inept governments in Eastern Europe, Spain, and South America, and the Germans were hedging on making scheduled reparations payments under the Dawes Plan. As if things weren't bad enough, the heavyweight boxing championship was vacant, the Pulitzer Committee found no work meritorious enough to receive a prize in reporting, and in the tenth year since Wilson's great crusade, the Nobel Committee awarded no peace prize.

Most Americans glanced at those depressing headlines, then turned quickly to escapism with Al Jolson and Ruby Keeler, Chris Cagle, Reigh Count, Arnold Rothstein, or the Gumps. Few, however, could ignore the melancholy events of the Presidential campaign of 1928. Iowa Republican Herbert Hoover colorlessly jousted with the dead dragons of the League of Nations, the need for prohibition, government regulation of business. New York Democrat Al Smith insisted he was "going to beat the pants off Hoover." Nobody really believed him, though. Despite his popularity in his home state, where he had won the governor's chair four times, Smith was running against practically all the major trends in the nation.

As an antiprohibitionist, "Al-cohol" Smith, as his opponents dubbed him, had aroused a wide cross section of Americans. The old puritanical groups like the Anti-

Saloon League and the Women's Christian Temperance Union, Southern Baptists like Alabama's senator Tom Heflin, Northern Methodists like Coolidge's former attorny general Mrs. Mabel Willebrandt, the National Lutheran Editors Association, Dr. Hugh Walker of *The Presbyterian Magazine,* Dr. Henry Sloane Coffin of the Union Theological Seminary, and Dr. Bob Jones of Bob Jones University, the *Fellowship Forum,* the *Rail Splitter, The Voice,* and the *North Carolina Yellow Jacket*— all suggested that Smith wanted to make America "100% Catholic, Drunk and Illiterate."[1] Such charges were reinforced by a nationwide whispering campaign that implied the governor had disgraced himself publicly by reeling about in an inebriated condition at both the New York State Fair and a chautauqua in Indiana that September.[2]

As a product of New York's lower East Side, the Battery District under the towers of the Brooklyn Bridge, Smith evoked the snobbery of middle-class Americans, who felt this "Happy Hooligan" was better suited to the Fulton Fish Market than the White House. Often as not, his speech was studded with pithy illustrations ("an eye as glassy as a dead cod," "giving the feel of shaking hands with a frozen mackerel") culled from his experience as a worker in that same fish market.[3] At the same time, his pronunciation astounded America's heartland. With his slushy lapses into "deres," "doses," "foists," and "poisonallys," the governor could have recited the Gettysburg Address over the "raddio" and would have had people living west of the Hudson River puzzling whether he were in fact an American.

Additionally, Smith bore the stigma of Tammany

Hall, and all that that organization conjured up in terms of prostitution, vice, gambling, and liquor. Even the Kansas liberal William Allen White blistered Smith as "a dresser with pink and crimson tie who took orders from Tammany until he was able to give orders." [4] Smith was a Wet, an internationalist, an advocate of immigration reform, a fop and a slob at the same time, and much too citified for most Americans in 1928. And, finally, he was a Catholic, "the most fervently religious man I ever met," according to his adviser and friend, Judge Joseph Proskauer.[5]

Smith's religion was a fatal mark, for throughout the 1920s, wherever men contested for Congressional or Presidential seats, the shadow of the Invisible Empire of the Ku Klux Klan cast its leprous pall. Eight million affirmed, dues-paying bigots, sustained by a welter of frantic Fundamentalists, teetotalers, and nativists, resented and actively resisted legitimate efforts of aliens, Jews, blacks, or Catholics to blend into America's sociopolitico-economic system. The KKK and its sympathizers cost Smith the Presidential nomination of the Democratic Party in 1924. Though weakened by scandal and a temporary resurgence of common sense in the country, a fragmented Klan could still play upon residual fears and hates of "good Americans" to frustrate Smith's ambitions once the nomination was his in 1928.[6] That fall, 10,000,000 anti-Catholic handbills, pamphlets, and leaflets flooded the nation, reviving vicious tales of convent life that had circulated during the Know Nothing era, charging that Catholics were against freedom, that the public schools would be Romanized, all civil marriages disallowed, the Vatican transferred to Washington if Smith were elected.[7] Herbert Hoover, himself the victim of a mild whispering campaign because of his Quaker background, disavowed such hate literature.[8] And, for the most part, Smith, who had affirmed his belief in democracy, freedom of religion, and the necessity of separating church and state in an open letter to *The Atlantic* in May 1927, tried to ignore it.[9]

Shortly after Labor Day, and bolstered by George Peek, Hugh Johnson, and Rexford Tugwell, who filled him in on the McNary-Haugen surplus equalization fee plan, Smith trudged off aboard a special whistlestopping train to prove he could relate to the people of Middle America. Wherever he went—Indianapolis, Omaha, Denver, Helena, Saint Paul, Milwaukee—the emphasis in his colloquies was on federal subsidies to farmers, the need for public power, greater vision from the federal government. There were the nagging rumors about his drinking and religion, and the governor was somewhat distracted by the need to name a successor at the upcoming state convention, but, like Wilson, Smith believed he had captured the imagination of rural America. As the eleven-car train carrying the Presidential hopeful neared Oklahoma City on the evening of September 19, however, it was greeted by a double cordon of wooden crosses, blazing sentinels stretching out for hundreds of yards on either side of the right-of-way through the stockyards of Packingtown. The Klan was welcoming Al Smith to Oklahoma.[10]

One hundred thousand quiet, sullen persons were waiting around Union Station on West Choctaw Street when Smith arrived. They did not approve of the loudspeakers that blared his theme song, "The Sidewalks of New York." Nor did they react enthusiastically to the little candidate with the brown derby hat. From afar, Smith's family in Manhattan listened to radio descriptions of his reception in Oklahoma City and feared for his safety. Later, Smith himself confided that the crowd posed "a hostility he had rarely encountered in all his experiences." [11] Whisked to a hotel by federal agents assigned to protect him, the governor spent the night arguing with advisers and local Democratic politicians who counseled him not to pick up the gauntlet thrust at him by the Klan.

Al Smith was not one to run away from a fight. A blunt, direct man with no patience with lying, cheating, or "skullduggery," he exchanged a number of four-letter words with aides during the night. To Charles Michelson of the *New York World,* his chief ghostwriter, he confided that he would feel like a coward, unfit for any public office, if he were to permit these scurrilous attacks to go unanswered. He reminded his advisers how he had reacted when, during the gubernatorial campaign of 1924, Klansmen had burned a cross in Ithaca, New York, one night after he had spoken in that city. Of the KKK, Smith had said then: "To my mind, the whole movement is out of line with the spirit of our free institutions. It is so out of tune with the history and purposes of this country, it is so abhorrent to intelligent, thinking Americans of all denominations, that it must in time fall to the ground of its own weight. The Catholics of the country can stand it. The Jews can stand it. Our citizens born under foreign skies can stand it. But the United States of America cannot stand it. Nor can they countenance a policy of silence in regard to it on the part of the man who has a special commission to speak for one heart and conscience of the American people." [12]

Smith's sketchy notes in preparation for this major speech demonstrate two things: (a) his ability to speak with clarity and at length on any subject with the tersest of notes and (b) the great inner turmoil he felt. He had wanted to address national issues, explain his record, but his outline shows that he felt compelled to speak about "Mrs. Willebrandt, who is she," "cry of Tammany is red herring," "what lies behind religion," "discuss and denounce whispers," "challenge truth and sincerity," and "Jeffersonian Democracy and American Liberty." [13]

On the evening of Thursday, September 20, 1928, as he prepared to enter the Oklahoma City Coliseum, a more hesitant Smith told speechwriter Michelson, "I'm scared, Charlie. I'm wondering how it will go. I don't know those people out there. I don't speak their language." [14]

It is questionable whether Smith was communicating with any of the 10,000 people assembled in the livestock exposition hall, at first. For ten minutes he told of how he had championed increases in teacher salaries and building appropriations for all kinds of schools (especially in rural sections of New York State), how he had opposed censorship of the kind entailed in the Lusk bills (which would have required loyalty oaths of teachers in New York State), how he had pushed for an annual expenditure of $10,000,000 for hospital and prison construction, why he favored public control of the water power of the Hudson and Saint Lawrence rivers, how he had established a State Housing Board with extensive powers to foster low-cost public housing, how through the genius of Robert Moses he had instituted a state system of public parks stretching from Niagara to Montauk Point, how he had introduced the first governor's cabinet in his state's history, and how he had revamped the civil service system.

When Smith went on to extol the Democratic Party as the party of Wilson and Cleveland, of liberty and justice for the common man, many of his listeners in the poorly ventilated hall nodded more from ennui than agreement. Then, suddenly, he lashed out against those claques, the superpatriots, the 100 percent Americans, the Klan, who threatened to destroy freedom in America. Singling out the Klan for special attention as totally ignorant of Americanism and a menace to itself and the nation, Smith spat; "If there are any considerable number of our people that are going to listen to appeals to their passion and their prejudice, if bigotry and intolerance and their sister vices are going to succeed, it is dangerous for the future of the Republic, and the best way to kill anything un-American is to drag it out into the open, because anything un-American cannot live in sunlight."

As a few bib-overalled Sooners shouted, "Pour it on 'em, Al!" Smith continued, "Just think of a man breathing the spirit of hatred against millions of his fellow citizens proclaiming himself to be an American and proclaiming and subscribing at the same time to the doctrine of Jefferson, of Lincoln, of Roosevelt, of Wilson."

There was no deliberate East Side mispronunciation nor any mistaking the allusion to his welcome to Oklahoma as Smith went on angrily, "Why there is no greater mockery in this world today than the burning of the cross, the emblem of salvation, the place upon which Christ himself made the great sacrifice for all of mankind, by these people who are spreading this propaganda, while the Christ that they are supposed to adore, love and venerate all of his lifetime on earth taught the holy, sacred writ of brotherly love. Nothing could be so out of line with the spirit of America. Nothing could be so foreign to the teachings of Jefferson. Nothing could be so contradictory to our whole history. Nothing could be so false to the teachings of our Divine Lord Himself." [15]

Despite fear of personal harm, Smith had courageously delivered his one formal denunciation of bigotry in the Presidential campaign. He need not have fretted over its impact. Oklahoma City yawned at the New Yorker with the bow tie, and packed the same auditorium the very next night to hear Dr. John Roach Straton, resident minister of the New York City Calvary Baptist Church, continue his Fundamentalist crusade against "card-playing, cocktail drinking, poodle dogs, divorce, novels, stuffy rooms, dancing, evolution, Clarence Darrow, overeating, nude art, prize fighting, actors, greyhound racing, modernism, Al Smith and the Forces of Hell." [16] Six weeks later, Oklahomans would reject Smith in the Presidential referendum, 394,046 to 219,174.

H. L. Mencken might attribute the first defeat of a Democrat in Oklahoma in this century to the inherent yokelism of the residents of that state. Self-proclaimed sophisticates have always imputed qualities of bigotry and stupidity to the South and Midwest. These same critics would have more difficulty in rationalizing the resurrection of a mendacious religious canard in Smith's own home state just two days after the governor's eloquent plea for tolerance halfway across the country. In Massena, New York, where the Ku Klux Klan burned seven crosses that year, the cool fall weekend of September 22–23 was to be one of grief, hatred, and insanity.

2

*I*t would have taken the better part of a day for someone in a Nash 400 or a Whippet Six to make the 200-mile journey along Routes 12 and 37 from Syracuse to Massena, New York, in the fall of 1928. As one left behind the ghosts of St. Leger, Montgomery, Arnold, and Burgoyne, winding macadam roads, alternating with dangerously slippery patches of blacktop, would take him through endless reaches of unattractive beeches, birches, hickorys, and mountain ash, all of which seemed to have been tossed together in a mockery of nature's general preference for symmetry. Driving along the stark scrub-infested southern side of the Saint Lawrence River, the tourist would have gained a new appreciation for the oft-expressed desire of so many Americans to invade and annex Canada in the nineteenth century. The purity and deep green of the

Canadian side contrasted vividly with the tawdry vacation cottages, lemonade stands, and filling stations that pocked the road from Alexandria Bay to Massena. The hundred yards of mud-gray water that separated the two nations seemed to represent something more than a territorial line—perhaps the visions of discontented dairy farmers on this side of the river and their tranquil counterparts in Ontario.[1]

In reality, this North Country Division, as geographers call upper New York State, was little more than an extension of French Canada. Geologically, its limestone and sandstone bases are more akin to the general configuration found from Kingston to Saint Lambert than that of Dutchess County or Albany, from which it is shielded by the craggy Adirondacks.[2] Its climate, seven months of winter, as some joked after suffering through 150 inches of snow and several collapsed roofs in 1970 and 1977, likewise is a reflection of that endured by people in Montreal or Ottawa. It may be that harsh winters have merely reinforced the will of those hardy folk who settled in Massena and refused to let Indians or nature chase them away. The various nationalities that peopled Massena came for a variety of reasons and over a century and a half.

At the end of the American Revolution, the New York Legislature, desperate for funds to pay off wartime debts, created a board of land commissioners under the direction of Governor George Clinton. The commission was empowered to sell the state's public lands. In 1787, surveys were carried out and the commissioners put up for sale two ranges of five townships, each ten miles square, in what was to become the state's largest county, Saint Lawrence County.[3] At the time, there was little to entice settlers to such an isolated region. Even today, an American twisting his radio dial for a program in English feels somewhat detached from his own society because of the preponderance of French in the area. That is not surprising when one considers that the closest city of any import to Massena, Roosevelttown, Potsdam, Waddington, or Canton is not even in the United States. Ottawa is 80 miles northwest of Massena Circle via the Ogdensburg bridge. Montreal lies 90 miles to the northeast. The remoteness of the community, perched as it is practically at the top of the United States, was even more pronounced at the beginning of the nineteenth century, when residents of Massena had to tramp 120 miles east to transact business at the county seat of Plattsburgh.

In addition to isolation, inclement weather, plagues of grasshoppers and freakish insects derisively called Canadian soldiers, and hostile French trappers, settlers in the Northern Country had to contend with the Saint Regis Indians. Counted among the Iroquois nations, this tribe had been converted to Christianity by the French nobleman-priest John Francis Regis early in the seventeenth century. Under provisions of a treaty signed May 31, 1796, the Indians were removed to a six square mile reservation at Hogansburg. From their straggling, unpainted cabins in Akwis-as-ne ("where the partridge drums"), or Indian Meadows, the Saint Regis Indians continued to claim all land along the Grasse and Raquette rivers 20 miles to the west. When their protests against a 1799 state patent to Jeremiah Van Rensselaer for the development of what were to become Massena and Louisville townships proved ineffective, the Indians retaliated by shooting any cattle found straying onto reservation land. By 1928, the once-proud tribe had dwindled to 2,800 (including fewer than 100 full-blooded Indians), living at subsistence level from the sale of handmade baskets and moccasins.[4]

Ironically, Massena may owe its name and growth to two of those factors that should have deterred Anglo-American settlement—namely, the French and Indians. In 1792, Anable Fancher, a French-Canadian from Montreal seeking a site for a sawmill and appreciating the power potential of the 90-foot drop along the banks of the American side of the Saint Lawrence River (since developed into the Moses Saunders Power Dam and the Bertrand Snell and Dwight Eisenhower locks of the Saint Lawrence Seaway), leased a mile from the Indians along the Grasse River and created a bustling log cabin settlement. By 1800, this community had come to be known as Massena.

No one knows who was responsible for the name, but all indications point to someone of French origin, perhaps Fancher himself. Though most people associate the name with Italian cities of similar pronunciation, Massena was actually named after Andreé Masséna, Duke of Rivoli, Marshal of the Empire, recipient of the Legion of Honor, and, in the words of the town's Chamber of Commerce, "who most historians would agree was Napoleon Bonaparte's greatest general."[5] Most historians would take issue with the exaggerated significance of the general who once plotted with Count Jean Baptiste Jules Bernadotte to overthrow Napoleon, who lived quite nicely with his ladies while on campaign, and who performed like a Gilbert and Sullivan model major general during Napoleon's Iberian fiasco. Still, French-Canadians in the New World must have been sufficiently impressed with Masséna's role in the Alps, Italy, the Rhineland, and Switzerland from 1792 to 1799.[6] After the fall of Napoleon, some Massenans wanted to change the town's name to Jefferson or Americus or Liberty, but all such efforts failed. Poor old Marshal Masséna died a few years later in Paris, unaware, and probably uncaring, that a town somewhere in the wilds or North America had been named for him.

Through the nineteenth century, Massena's growth was slow. Several more sawmills were constructed, while the lumber jacks ravaged lush forests to the west. Woolen mills, tanneries, cooper and cabinet shops, and rickety structures with steeples sprang up in the village center as Massena began to resemble those quasi-ghost towns in the nation's Northeast that limp on through economic atrophy. Every ten or twenty years the timbers straddling the Grasse River rotted or were washed away in a spring flood and the villagers appropriated another $1,000 for "the bridge." It was not until after World War I that Massena's principal streets—Main, Orvis, Andrews, Maple—could be paved.[7]

If the villagers enjoyed little prosperity, at least farmers in outlying areas knew better times. By the Civil War, Saint Lawrence County was the second largest milk-producing area in the state. Although the land was neither as rich nor as attractive as that of Wisconsin dairy centers, people in the North Country prided themselves on their Holsteins and Herefords and shipped out as much as 50,000,000 pounds of milk and cream to New York City each year. By 1945, the Diamond Creamery Company alone was shipping two carloads of butter to Boston and other New England markets every Monday morning.[8] For a handful of dairy farmers who could maintain the pace and invest in modern equipment, such demand meant a modicum of affluence.

Such affluence, however, was late in arriving and left most villagers unaffected. Massenans needed a gimmick, some sort of special attraction to put the town on the map, invite fresh investment. Here the Indians came to the assistance of the white inhabitants. For a long time, it had been known that the Saint Regis tribe had used the water of the Raquette (also known as Racket) River for medicinal purposes. As early as 1815, it is reported, some whites began seeking relief from skin ulcerations and other cutaneous diseases in the sulfurous water "that comes out of the ground, smells bad, but cures sick animals and sick Indians when they lick it." In 1822, Captain John Polley, a resident of Massena since 1803, purchased forty acres on the banks of the Racket. Envisioning Massena as a health spa, there, at what is now the corner of East Hatfield and Main streets, on the village's extreme eastern limits, Polley raised a lodge to accommodate health seekers.

According to an article published in *Harper's New Monthly Magazine* many years later, about the time

Polley established his first hostel on the Racket, "a young girl, afflicted with salt-rheum, came and was completely healed. A few years later, the Canadian Roman Catholic Bishop, Alexander McDonald, came with the black scrofula which he had contracted in Egypt. His legs were covered with black ulcers to the knees. He remained a month and was completely cured. Since then, hundreds afflicted with every description of cutaneous disease, chronic dyspepsia and diarrhea and kindred ailments have found relief or positive cures."

Once Polley had shown the way to exploiting the natural springs of the Racket, other entrepreneurs enlarged upon his venture. The warm waters were sheltered by an ornate covered platform. Public bathhouses were constructed, along with a number of hastily built resort lodges, some of which still stand. Dominating the entire scene, however, were Harrowgate House and the United States Hotel, built in 1828 and 1848, respectively, and both of which came under the control of Benjamin Phillips before the Civil War. When the latter hotel burned in 1871, it was replaced by the elegant, $75,000 Hatfield House. This three-storied mansion, with its circumscribed porch, innumerable gables, omnipresent Victorian tower and widow's walk, was the pride of a Massena that hoped to rival Saratoga, Clifton, Lebanon, Richfield, Chittenango, and Sharon for the dollars of the gullible and invalid.[9]

By 1900, Massena's health boomlet was played out. Distance had proved fatal, along with delay in pushing a railroad line north. The town's population stagnated at around 1,000. Most of the health grifters were dead, their properties deteriorating. For a time, Hatfield House served as an apartment building, then as a storehouse, until it finally burned down in December 1932. Many old-timers clung to the hope of reviving the glories of Massena Springs in the Gilded Age. After World War I, some thought was given to the development of the Springs property as a sanitarium for the care of disabled veterans. The state rejected the idea. As late as 1937, the New York Legislature authorized an inquiry into the health potential of mineral waters at different spots, including Massena. The special committee concluded that *if* the state of New York "at some future time" expanded its public health services to include the development of mineral spring recreational resorts, *then* Massena Springs should be given "most careful consideration." Thirty-four years after that recommendation, nothing had been done. Yet the Massena Chamber of Commerce continued to dream. "Someday we may have the local mineral springs built back to where it was a number of years ago." [10]

Massena's fortune always lay in its water, and with the decline of the health spa at the turn of the century, other potential sources of revenue had to be explored. In 1895, Henry Warren and M. H. Flaherty of Massena, C. A. Kellogg of Ogdensburg, and engineers Albon Man and Charles Higgins of New York City chartered the Saint Lawrence Power Company of Massena. The purpose of this group was to harness 200,000 horsepower of water-generated energy by cutting a canal from the Saint Lawrence River rapids over three miles to the Grasse River. In 1898, the T. A. Gillespie Company of Pittsburgh took over the contract for excavation of the 25-foot-deep, 300-foot-wide ditch. Later in the year, Gillespie's brother, David, a director of the Pittsburgh Reduction Company (later called the Aluminum Company of America—Alcoa), visited Massena and reported favorably back to his associates that here in the north was the kind of cheap hydroelectric power essential to the production of aluminum. In August 1903, Alcoa's first smelting plant, employing 63 persons, opened in Massena. Since then, Alcoa's works have mushroomed into a veritable sister city of Massena, with more than fifty acres of warehouses, mills, shops, and forges turning out aluminum pig, ingot, wire, rod, bar, structural shapes, electrical conductor cable, and covered conductor cable, while providing jobs for more than 3,000 Massenans. After the completion of the Saint Lawrence Seaway locks in 1954, Alcoa was joined by Reynolds Metals and Chevrolet, both of which established super plants in the area.[11]

This economic revitalization of Massena was, nonetheless, painfully slow. By 1928 there were only 8,500 residents in the village proper, fewer than 12,000 in that peculiar geographic subdivision that New Yorkers refer to as the town (and that in the Western Reserve is known as a township). While the population figures were not striking, the makeup of those who came to work in the mills or live off the mills was. Dozens of immigrant Italian families settled in Little Italy, north of the Grasse River on Main Street. More Polish immigrants came and took over the Polish Grove to the northeast. Still shy of manpower necessary to operate its plants in the prosperous 1920s, Alcoa secured legal dispensation from the Alien Contract Labor Law (the statute dating back to 1885 that barred the importation of foreign labor if such immigration was tied to a previously contracted job) and tantalized many French-speaking Canadians across the border.[12] The Bourdons, Langloises, Perrottes, Michauds, Guimonds, Guyettes, Carrieres, Bourdeaus, St. Germains, Plantes, Thibaults, and Tousignants who came to Massena were only part of a general exodus of more than 80,000 people who settled in a French-Canadian, Roman Catholic belt from Massena to the Vermont border before 1940.[13]

A few Greeks came, and as if mocking their own stereotype, opened restaurants in Massena's business district. There, they shared the village's retail trade with Jews, many of whom were recent arrivals from the ghettos of Eastern Europe. Despairing of the noisome street competition along New York's Lower East Side, they made the long hegira northward seeking a region where they were "not tied down by prejudices, laws or a Pale," where farmers would react favorably to their baskets of nonessentials like ribbon, thread, toothbrushes, suspenders, pins and needles, and which was "least infested by his colleagues."[14] The Jews seem to have found such a friendly, open, tolerant community in Massena. "Heinz 57" nationalities and religions lived together in peace and friendship in this town, which was a microcosm of the great American Melting Pot.

In frustrations, ethnic animosity, and lightly repressed vigilantism, Massena was a mirror of the United

States in 1928. Although the town was overwhelmingly
Republican and its citizens extremely scrupulous about
church attendance, Republican-sponsored Prohibition
presented many with a moral dilemma. Even a 140-
pound weakling could row a boatload of blended whis-
key across the narrow Saint Lawrence at Louisville
Landing or Fort Covington. Such temptations apparently were too much, for rarely did an issue of the
Massena Observer come out without word of a bootleg-
ger's being shot by immigration officers at Duane Center or some Massenan being detained for illegal posses-
sion of spirits. The region did, after all, have a history of
rebellion dating back to Jefferson's ill-fated Embargo
Act of 1808. At that time, defiant pioneers, denied their
principal income, which came from the sale of potash in
Canada, would send rafts of material floating into the
Saint Lawrence or would topple primitive huts filled
with potash off cliffs into the neighboring land.[15] In
1928, most old-time Massenans disdained such extrale-
gal activity, opting instead to serve as clerks, postmen,
policemen, firemen, or as handymen about town and on
the farms. Some, holding such employment to be beneath their dignity, absolutely refused to enter the mills.
And this led to another problem.

Massena's Anglo-Saxon Protestants feared that their
homogeneous community, its standards and values,
were being undermined by Catholics, Greeks, and other
aliens. They might wink at the story of the "Frenchie"
who, upon hearing that the School Board had no
cuspidor, nominated Jean Giron "for cuspidor." They
also might laugh at the story of the other "Frenchie"
who won a new Chevrolet in a lottery. Lacking furni-

ture or electricity in his hut, he simply cut a hole through the wall and drove the vehicle into his living room. Now he could read by the auto's lights, listen to its radio, cook meals on the engine, and sleep on its comfortable upholstery.[16] Much as these stories confirmed their own superiority, the "townies" resented economic advantages enjoyed by the newcomers. An old-time Massenan, whose grandfather or father had fought for liberty in the Civil War, might labor at some "honorable" job and bring home no more than $15 per week. A semiskilled French-Canadian, on the other hand, no more than six weeks in the country, and unable to speak anything but an unintelligible foreign garble, might draw as much as $25 or $50 per week from Alcoa. Then, to make matters worse, these foreigners (supposedly dark, handsome, and seductive) [17] would flash their bankrolls along Main Street, buying up all the natty alpaca, worsted, or "cassimere" suits that were available for $18.95 at Kniff's, Levine's, Kauffman's, Schine's, Clopman's, Fishman's, or Sperling's.

The natives might resent the influx of Poles, Italians, Lithuanians, Yugoslavs, and Canucks, and the threat of popery in Saint Lawrence County might have disquieted some Massenans, but nothing grated against them as much as the presence and power of nineteen Jewish families in town.[18] The Jews were, after all, latecomers to Massena, the first, Jesse Kauffman, having arrived only in 1898. When they huddled in yarmulke and tallis for their Herbrew prayers in the old Second Congregational Church, renamed Adath Israel after its purchase in 1919, they resembled not so much good Christian congregants as sinistral wizards from a tale by the brothers Grimm. Who, passing the eighty-year-old red-brick structure late in August, could fail to be disturbed by the weird lamentations and chants emanating from the open door and window? How should a Gentile know that this was the observance of Tishah-b'-Ab, that mournful day that commemorates the destruction of the Solomonic Temple, The Temple of Herod, the defeat of Simon Bar Kochba and the expulsion from Spain? To the average Massenan scurrying up West Orvis, davening (physical, rocking prayer) might be a danse macabre, the Jews' cries invocations to Satan, the *Ner Tamid* (eternal light before the Ark) a beacon for that creature's way.

The Jewish community in Massena was an anomalous one, geographically and socially isolated. It was, moreover, a relatively prosperous one, as the signs above the most prominent furniture, jewelry, and clothing stores on Main Street attested. Massena's Jews lived quietly, a quiet bred in the shtetl and ghetto. They worked hard—*areuf arbetn zich* (get ahead, better yourself) was the motto of the immigrant Jew. Even more than their Gentile counterparts in this hardy climate, they demonstrated *gvure* (fortitude) when their children told them of Christmas trees and Christmas carols in classrooms, of the Lord's Prayer in assemblies, Easter vacations, and teachers who lectured their pupils that anyone who was not a Christian was a pagan.[19] *Gvure* meant shrugging a Jewish shrug when one of their neighbors insisted that Christ was not a Jew. What was he, then? A Christian, of course. You had to get along, improve yourself. As a mark of good business sense, then, but also to vitiate incipient anti-Semitism, the owners of Kauffman's, Friedman, Rosenbaum and Stone's, or Shulkin and Slavin's extended credit to their customers in an age of cash purchase. Jacob Shulkin and Sam Slavin even posted bail bonds for many unfortunates snared in Prohitition dragnets along the Saint Lawrence. The last two men were also instrumental in the creation of the first Chamber of Commerce in April 1930.

The Jewish merchants would have been amazed and sorrowed if they had known the extent of resentment that their prosperity had generated among those they tried to befriend. Marie Elden-Brown, a sweet, diminutive woman, who for forty-seven years served as the leader of the town's Girl Scout troop, and who in 1928 had been residing in Massena for three years since coming from England, commented, "It was a sneaky anti-Semitism, not the open kind. But I think this type is the more dangerous." In crisp, British tones, Mrs. Elden-Brown, onetime town historian, added, "There were all kinds of snide remarks made in groups, behind people's backs, the kind of remarks that I was not used to in my country. I recall one man who was in my home. He started to talk like that. I told him, 'I have three doors in this house. You may have your pick and leave.' It was an attitude of 'who cares about the Jews.' For example, we have cemetery records for Baptists, Catholics, Methodists, et cetera, but when I became town historian in 1965, I was surprised to learn that no records had ever been kept for our Jewish population. When I checked around, I was appalled at the reaction of officials who really did not want to be bothered."[20]

THE INCIDENT AT MASSENA

With its anti-Semitism, anti-alienism, and anti-Catholicism, Massena was no different from any number of little towns across the country in 1928. As in Poland, Niles or Berea, Ohio, Chester, Pennsylvania, Dearborn, Michigan, or Asheville, North Carolina, old-stock Americans sought comfort with their fellow bigots in the Ku Klux Klan. How strong the Klan may have been in Massena is hard to determine. Seward Hanmer, a beak-nosed man who was in his teens then, and who later became one of the more prominent attorneys in town, maintains that while there was always a Klavern, its members did little but talk. Others maintain that as many as forty to fifty Massenans were active in the Klan and participated at cross-burnings at Waterman Hill in Canton, 30 miles south.[21] When setting out on their night-riding escapades, these self-proclaimed vigilantes wore normal Klan regalia. Such hoods and gowns really weren't necessary, though, as the townsfolk generally knew who was hiding beneath the sheets. Cole Cummins, now ninety-three years old and quite alert, a lifelong Massena resident and a former clerk at Alcoa, recalls that one of the Klansmen who attempted to disguise himself was Willard Countryman. An elderly, stocky, "pussy" little man who came to the United States from Canada around the turn of the century, Countryman had been a failure at everything he had tried. Sharecropper, town handyman, common laborer, he was perfect fodder for the Klan and its demonology. He was, however, cursed with a distinctively awkward gait, which prompted Cummins to say, "Old Willard Countryman was one of them that would come into town under those sheets. Everyone knew it was him.

Hell! I could have told his walk even if he wore a fur
coat off a bear."[22]

In its rare moments of honesty, the Klan convoked
public meetings at the Advent Church on the corner of
West Orvis and Andrews. If fortunate to secure the
services of an itinerant spellbinder from downstate, it
might even rent out the third-story meeting hall on
Main Street that was normally used by the Masons. It
was to just such a meeting that Jacob Shulkin was
invited in 1928. Mike Scheetz, a workman from the Ball
Coal Company (located next to Shulkin's store on
Water Street), apparently ignorant either of the Klan's
position on Judaism or Shulkin's Jewish background,
told him, "Jake, you gotta go. This is the finest thing
that's ever happened in this country. The Klan is really
going to wake up the country. It's going to save America
for guys like you and me. You gotta join."

Flattered, and somewhat bemused, Shulkin responded, "Sorry, Mike, I can't."

"Why not?"

"I won't ever qualify," cracked the Jewish shop-
keeper. "You have to be a one hundred percent prick to
join the Klan, Mike, and I'm not."[23]

Because he was a Mason, and because he was blessed
with the quality of courage that Jews call chutzpah,
Shulkin did attend the Klan rally. He was accompanied
by his nineteen-year-old son, Ben, at that time the sole
Jewish student at Clarkson Institute in Potsdam. Ben
was a young man who believed the KKK was something one read about in history books or saw in a D. W.
Griffith epic. He soon realized his mistake, along with
several hundred men, women, and children who lis-

tened to the shrill speech of a missionary from Saranac Lake. Saranac Lake was Al Smith's summer retreat, and who better than a preacher from that community to expose the conspiracy of godless Jews and papists to enslave America through the vehicle of Al Smith? The only way to prevent this takeover was to join the Klan and combat the forces of evil and anarchy.

When the sermonette was ended and Massenans began to make their way to those tables where membership in the Klan might be secured (for a price), Jacob Shulkin stood and implored his neighbors to disregard the invective they had heard. It was to no avail, as his son, Ben, recalls: "The people were all lining up to join." In fact, this courageous gesture may have jeopardized the lives of all those in the Shulkin household. Perhaps it was the fact that the slope leading away from the rear of the Shulkins' houses on Maple Street down to the Grasse River was visible in the downtown section of Massena. Perhaps it was just coincidence. But one of the seven crosses burned in Massena that fall was set ablaze in Jacob Shulkin's backyard.

No one was ever apprehended for that atrocity. Indeed, there is no record of any Klansman's ever being punished for any act in Massena. Klan literature mysteriously materialized in the boxes of postal patrons, and Postmaster J. B. Andrews, a martinet whose concern for efficiency in postal operations was well known, but who was also a staunch American patriot,[24] declined to act upon complaints. Obscene diatribes against Presidential hopeful Al Smith and huge red crosses appeared suddenly on the side walls of downtown businesses (the swastika was not yet in favor as an international symbol of bigots), and Massena's six-man police force did nothing. Massena's officials, its mayor, councilmen, supervisors, firemen, like the gathering of Protestant ministers of Saint Lawrence County that met in the Methodist Church on September 10 and denounced Al Smith for wanting to turn the clock of civilization backward,[25] merely winked at the Klan's activities. Beneath the facade of calm and toleration, Massena was a volcano of economic jealousy, prohibitionist and antiprohibitionist fanaticism, anti-Semitism, anti-Catholicism, anti-alienism, and assorted other mesozoic hatreds. All that was needed to release this pent-up fury was an excuse.

3

*I*t was three-thirty, September 22, 1928, an ordinary Saturday afternoon in Massena. The sky was clear, although there had been a trace of rain the previous night. Temperatures were in the low sixties. A nice fall day. The farmers who had come to town that morning to do their marketing had been gone for hours. The retail stores—Penney's, the Boston Store, and all the Jewish establishments that opened after Sabbath services—were still open, but few, if any, customers fondled the merchandise. Across from the Chesterfield billboard near Andrews and Orvis (once deemed scandalous because it portrayed a woman sitting on a hill with her lover, pleading with him to "blow some my way"), a few men stood and talked. Not about hurricanes in Florida or Al Smith's Oklahoma City speech. The fire that destroyed Fregoe's barn on Monday. Alcoa's being sued for the accidental death of a young man. The

woman in Cornwall who drowned her two infant children and then tried to kill herself by swallowing lye.

About this time, the town revived for a moment, as
dozens of blinking children, their eyes unaccustomed to
the light, came pouring out of the two movie theaters
downtown. It was Babe Ruth Day in Massena, and both
the Rialto and the Strand had promised every child who
attended the matinee of *Girl Shy,* starring Rex Bell, or
Pals in Peril, with Buffalo Bill, Jr., a Babe Ruth kite or a
flapper doll.[1]

The man was big and rugged. He was wearing simple
clothes, a somewhat frayed white shirt and gray wash
pants, symbols of the starched-collar proletariat of the
1920s. The little girl in the page-boy cut who walked by
his side holding his hand quite obviously was his daughter. Dave Griffiths and his four-year-old Barbara
trudged uphill along Andrews Avenue from Massena
Center to the modest green-and-white frame duplex at 8
Cherry Street that was home. It was a tiring, fifteen-
minute climb for the little girl, but the family could not
afford an automobile (and would not be able to buy one
until after the payment of Griffiths's World War I
bonus). Dave Griffiths was used to the walk. He made it
every morning—to catch a shuttle bus out to Alcoa.
Missing that bus meant he had to slog two or three
miles through hip-high snow or mud during the winter.[2]

Dave Griffiths looked down at the button-nosed child
with her big brown eyes and brown hair, and was
proud. He could never say no to his "Barbs." When she
begged to accompany him into town on a shopping
errand after her five-year-old brother, Bobby, and several of his friends had gone off to play in the nearby

woods without her, he could hardly refuse. First Bobby—the spitting image of him, people said—then Barbara—so much like her mom, with a voice like little bells chiming—and now a third child on the way. Marion Griffiths was five months pregnant. Things were not especially great for the Griffithses, but they were proud of what they had achieved in a few years. Dave was working regularly as a shipping clerk at Alcoa. His third year. The pay was not good, just $35 per week, but it did meet their needs.

Times had not always been even this good for the Griffithses. They had met and fallen in love twenty-five years earlier when both were students of Robert Frost at Derry, New Hampshire. There were complications, however. Marion Blood Griffiths, a tall, charming woman with granitelike features, still intelligent and beautiful at eighty-nine, was of old New England stock, replete with that peculiar diction that eschews the final *r* from all words. Dave was the son of a Richville, New York, bus driver. He had gained admission to the exclusive school only through the intervention of an uncle who was then serving as president of a small college in Hawaii.

This was no Romeo-and-Juliet affair with opposition from parents. Dave Griffiths wanted to make his own way in life, without any favors. While Marion completed a two year teacher-training course at Salem Normal College in Massachusetts, he attended Saint Lawrence University in Canton. In 1915, after several years of seeking his fortune with marble-works companies in Vermont, Colorado, and Texas, he returned to New York State and Massena. Two years later, he joined the AEF, and in 1921, almost twenty years after the romance had begun, he finally married his childhood sweetheart. The children they had longed for were twilight children, gifts of God to people who had sacrificed for one another in De Maupassant-like fashion until their late thirties.

Things would be better for the children, Dave told himself. Prices were going up. Everything seemed to be more expensive. Razor blades 35 cents a pack, coffee 45 cents a pound, cornflakes 22 cents, and new cars over at Payment Motor Sales more than $1,100. But the kids would get their educations and become true professional people. Bobby would not have his dreams of being an engineer exploded, would not have to work in a factory like his dad. And Barbara—Barbs would be a teacher like her mom. He squeezed her hand and smiled.

The little girl looked up and returned the grin. There was nobody in the world bigger, braver, or smarter than her daddy. She liked being with him, liked the way he showed her off to the world. Hers was a carefree world of celluloid dolls that said "Ma-ma," of dress-up for church, of the anticipation of going to school in another year just like her older brother Bobby. The two were only fourteen months apart, but between them there was none of the sibling animosity that normally marks such a relationship. "They always played together," said Dave Griffiths. "They were very close." Barbara Griffiths clutched two lollipops in her free hand—one for herself and one for her brother. She just wished that it wasn't such a long way back home.

Father and daughter turned the corner of Allen Street

and walked along the gutters of Cherry Street. There were no sidewalks. They entered the side door and found Marion Griffiths in the kitchen. Theirs was not an impressive home—a few overstuffed chairs (wingless and slightly old-fashioned even for this period), a straight-back sofa, some polished wooden tables with pictures of Marion's parents, the inevitable wooden icebox. And there were several plants and flowers in the house, for both Dave and Marion enjoyed puttering in their small garden.

Dave Griffiths gave his wife a peck on the cheek.

"Was she a good girl?" Marion asked.

"Of course. Always. Right, Barbs?" He set a bag of groceries on the kitchen table. Barbara nodded in agreement.

"Mommy, can I have a sucker?"

Marion Griffiths looked at her husband, then back to the little girl, and said, "The boys just went back into the woods with a neighbor. They're looking to make whistles out of willow branches. Go fetch Bobby and then we'll give the two of you candy."

It was not an unusual request. Fifty yards south of the Griffiths' residence, and one was already into the swamp and pastureland that Massenans called the Nightingale Section (after the one farm that was situated here). Barbara knew her brother's favorite haunts within the tangled maples, birches, beeches, willows, goldenrod, Queen Anne's lace, purple ragweed, sumac, and burrs. She had been in and out of the Nightingale Section by herself since she was two years old and had never gone astray. There were some wild animals out there—skunks, porcupines, deer, and a few non-poisonous snakes—but nothing to worry about. A 500-pound black bear had been reported at Malone, Saint Regis Falls, and Tupper Lake recently, but there hadn't been any of them around Massena for as long as anyone could remember.[3] The Nightingale Section, with its lazy Herefords, its ponds perfect for skipping rocks, its boulders ideal for good-guys-versus-bad-guys ambushes, was a made-to-order recreation area for Massena's children, and was so favored by the Girl Scouts and Brownies who made annual hikes through the area, and by adolescent boys who had cook-outs and constructed shanty clubhouses here.[4] Long after 1928, a transient bricklayer whom townsfolk knew only as "Swede" Anderson would be discovered in one of these lean-tos, a rifle propped against his skull.[5] That suicide came much later. In 1928, the only potential danger to a child seemed to be if he or she disturbed a hive of hornets, and Barbara knew better than that. Neither Dave nor Marion Griffiths was concerned as their daughter skipped along Cherry Street and disappeared down the general path beyond Ransom Avenue. Barbara was wearing a gingham dress, a light-blue sweater, anklets, and a pair of shoes that sold for 95 cents in 1928.

Fortune played a sardonic game of hide-and-seek that day. Bobby and his companions emerged from the second-growth woods not more than a few feet from where Barbara had gone in moments before. When queried by his parents whether he had seen his sister, Bobby replied he had not. The boy was given his lollipop, and, for a time, the Griffiths gave the matter little further thought. Barbara would return before dusk. With the approach of the supper hour, Dave Griffiths decided to go into the woods after her himself. Sunset comes relatively early in the North Country in September, before seven o'clock, and if Barbara were lost in the woods, he would have a time locating her in the dense foliage.

Accompanied by Bobby and the neighborhood boys, Griffiths made a sweep in a southeasterly direction toward the low-lying section that then contained a sizable stagnant pond, and that has since been reclaimed for the Massena High School complex. The search lasted until well past 5:00 P.M., and no more than a square mile of the Nightingale Section had been covered.

Dave Griffiths is an even-tempered, moderate man, and his friends maintain it is impossible to rile him. Even today, possible high winds and electrical storms are not sufficient to deter this octogenarian from camping out with much younger comrades in the Adirondacks. That afternoon, however, as his search proved futile, Griffiths grew increasingly disturbed. "I wasn't so much worried about bears, or the pond, or any of the rumors that soon started," he says today. "I figured she laid down somewhere and got tired. The kids camped out frequently after that. But she wasn't quite four years old. And it was chilly, cold." With the boys, Griffiths returned to Cherry Street on the chance that Barbara, like her brother, had doubled back and somehow missed them. Still, there was no word of the child.

Now the Griffithses' neighbors—George Ure, the gruff Scotsman with a thick brogue who lived with his wife upstairs at 8 Cherry,[6] old Mr. Carton, a widower who loved Barbara as his own and who always seemed to have candy for her, the Taylors, who lived in the brown-frame duplex at 10 Cherry—offered assistance in the hunt. Some friends went through the half-completed house at the corner of Allen and Cherry streets in the hope that Barbara, like other neighborhood children, had wandered into the shell while her parents were distracted. Another roughed-in house being constructed on Allen Street, three doors down from Andrews Avenue, was also searched, to no avail. Neighbors even rummaged through their own basements against the possibility that Barbara was hiding, playing a joke, or had even fallen in by accident. Again, nothing.

At that point, someone, no one knows who, tripped the alarm in one of several fireboxes that had been set up around town when Massena modernized its firefighting system in 1916. It was in that year that the village councilors appropriated funds to purchase a truck to replace the antiquated hose reel and pumper that served members of the volunteer fire department. To assist these volunteers in determining the general location of a fire (since many had to be summoned from outlying areas), each section of town was assigned a specific number of blasts from the electronic horn sitting above the two-story brick fire station on Andrews Avenue. For some peculiar reason, the continuous discordant squawk that sounded over the village that afternoon in September 1928 was that of the department's special emergency distress signal.[7]

It wasn't long before the truck laden with five or six

early arrivals swung out of the sliding doors and south along Andrews, its sirens screeching and cars full of the curious following. Significantly, the driver of the truck was Roy Countryman. A fair-haired, slim man, a fraction short of six feet tall, he was one of two permanent attendants at the firehouse. Over the years, and especially since the new equipment had been obtained, it had been noted that the volunteers were notoriously lax about caring for their hose and pumper. Like children assigned the task of watering garden flowers and returning the hose to its proper coiled position, the volunteers would rush to a fire, do their duty, then toss the hoses back onto the truck like so many worms in a bucket. Precisely because of this, the village fathers hired two so-called fire truck drivers. The first to apply for and secure such a post was Roy Countryman.[8]

The pay, $20 per week, was not phenomenal when contrasted with what one could earn at Alcoa, but Countryman would never have qualified for factory employment. A thresher accident out on a farm some years before (he had slipped on a wet table where the grain was being fed) had ripped several toes off one of his feet, and he had walked with a noticeable limp thereafter. The disability led to his deferment from World War I and also impaired his chances of participating in the economic boomlet afterward. Countryman was named fire chief in 1924, a title more honorary than real. However, as premier fire truck driver, he was the central personality at the Massena Fire Department. And while there is no proof that Roy Countryman was a member of the Ku Klux Klan ("He was not an agitator," says Cole Cummins), it is recalled by old-time Massenans that Klan sympathies were often expressed at the fire-house and that not a few of the twenty-five or thirty volunteers were actual Ku Kluxers. Among those volunteer firemen who happened to be a leader of the KKK was Roy's own father, Willard, the man who walked like a "bear in bedsheets." [9]

Although the momentary absence of a child would not seem to warrant the immediate attention of the Fire Department, it was there, with its hook and ladder blocking passage along Cherry Street. So, too, were most of Massena's police force, including Chief Floyd San Jule and Officers Stanton Hutchins and Clifford Holcomb. Like Roy Countryman, San Jule was a farm boy who had been lured into public service by thoughts of security and prestige. The $25 weekly salary he received placed him low on the economic ladder, but at least San Jule could strut about town in the collarless blue gabardine with a Sam Browne belt and double row of brass buttons impressing people. A tall, hulking man with thinning hair, gray eyes, and puffy jowls that gave his head the shape of an inverted pear, San Jule was more at home trapping speeders than seeking out lost little girls. His monthly report to the Village Council that September would list thirty-six arrests, a veritable crime wave for such a small community, except that most of them were drunk drivers, or people who had been ticketed by himself or motorcycle faddist Hutchins for racing faster than twenty miles per hour through town.[10]

Some Massenans recall San Jule as a good man, reasonably rational, level-headed, despite the weight of additional problems caused by rum-running along the border.[11] Others cringe at the mention of his name, putting him down in the words of Chamber of Commerce secretary Ernest Wagar as "stupid" or worse.[12] Town historian Marie Elden-Brown remembered San Jule as "a bully of a man," "a gun-happy cop," who was involved in a fatal shooting during a Prohibition raid out on the Scheetz farm in 1925.[13]

Perhaps the fairest assessment of the man who went on to become sheriff of Saint Lawrence County is that he was neither so good nor so bad as some have indicated, but merely mediocre, the stereotypical law-enforcement officer out of one of Hollywood's old Charlie Chan epics. He made no effort to combat Klan activities in town. He kept no regular blotter until April 1929, following completion of a special course of instruction at the New York State Police School at Troy.[14] After six weeks, the chief would receive a diploma certifying his qualifications for police work and another certifying his expertise in Red Cross first aid and lifesaving. Armed with those credentials, San Jule would return to Massena to conduct seminars for officers from surrounding village in "penal law," "conditions under which arrests can be made," "finding and following up clues," "laws governing motion pictures, dance halls and other forms of amusement," "arson," "common law," and "the handling of explosives." [15] Called upon to conduct a formal inquiry into any serious matter, San Jule would have been hopelessly ill-prepared.

San Jule must have been relieved to learn that Barbara Griffiths had disappeared beyond Ransom Avenue, the street demarking the village limits and his jurisdiction. Ultimate responsibility for her safe return would now devolve upon the two state troopers who were on permanent assignment to Massena from Company B in Malone. New York, in contrast with many neighboring states, apparently believing that visibility of troopers is a deterrent to crime, has always operated a number of such lonely substations. Today, these Highway Patrol quarters, generally converted old white saltboxes or village stores, can be seen throughout the northern part of the state. In 1928, though, patrolmen dispatched to Massena had to make do with a room in White's Hotel at the village center. If anything, the Spartan accommodations—two beds, a desk—were supposed to prompt the men to get on their patrols each morning.

Until the hotel barns at White's burned down in 1917, this meant mounting ponies supplied by the state and riding a circuit of the day's complaints. After World War I, troopers were given snappy little Ford Phaeton convertibles, which increased their mobility significantly. The one drawback with the Model A's was the standing order issued by Captain James Broadfield at the Malone barracks that the cars were never to have their tops up. In an age of rum-running and lawlessness, Broadfield reasoned, the troopers (resplendent in their Ranger-style hats, dark jackets, purple ties, olive breeches, and black puttees) must be seen at all times. The man who put up his canvas in subzero weather ran the risk of being fined for such an offense.[16]

There was a conscious effort made to create a myth about the troopers, their ability and intelligence. According to one popular legend, only those men tough enough to best the commanding officer in physical combat could qualify for Company B. Captain Broadfield, a big and robust man, propagandized visitors to the Malone barracks with tales of how troopers helped the poor "when they got a raw deal," how they were "kind to dumb criminals." [17] Everyone knew they attended the magnificent training school at Troy. Lamentably, apart from police officers in New York City, highway patrolmen (with their two months of books and firearms) were practically the only trained law-enforcement agents in the state.

Paragons of officiousness to this day, the troopers perpetuated their own image, not so much by actual accomplishment as through their sobriety and constant posturing. According to Carl Carmer, they swore "worse than loggers" and took pride not so much in dull patrol work as in their "Book of Horrors," a gruesome collection of murder cases solved by Company B. They especially loved to regale listeners with their capture of "Sambo," an insane black man who held off a dozen tough troopers until he had been riddled with bullets.[18] Comments that "Sambo" was a "vicious, gorilla-like" creature reinforced the impression offered by one former trooper, Joe Burke, that the men never did receive lessons in "etiquette in dealing with minorities." [19] More bluntly, another Massena resident adds, "New York troopers were not noted for their money or intellect at the time." [20]

Among the men of Company B was the senior trooper in Massena, Corporal Harry "Mickey" Mc-Cann. A short man, around five feet eight inches tall, with a ruddy complexion and a head of thick black hair,

McCann was known to his fellow officers as "a good, aggressive police officer, someone who could take the bull by the horns." [21] Single, in his thirties, he would serve twenty-five years on the force before retiring in the late 1940s as a sergeant. An Irish Catholic from Massachusetts, McCann possessed a high-school education. He was wounded in World War I and subsequently joined the Highway Patrol. On Monday, September 17, 1928, just five days before Barbara Griffiths' disappearance, McCann began his tour of duty in Massena with Trooper Ed Hughes.[22] McCann was as eager to impress Hughes, who was out on patrol for the first time, as he was bound to impress the townsfolk of Massena, with the excellence and efficiency of New York's state troopers.

When the two troopers pulled up outside the Griffiths residence around 5:40 P.M., Cherry Street was already aswarm with theories as to Barbara's whereabouts. Former police chief B. J. Demo kept maintaining that the little girl had merely lost her way and that she probably had just strayed farther than anyone had looked. Others conjectured that perhaps she had fallen into the great pond in Nightingale Section and drowned. Still others wondered whether she might have fallen over one of those many unseen rocks in the woods and either sprained an ankle or been knocked unconscious. The possibility of injury from animal attack was discounted. To Demo's suggestion that Barbara had wandered farther than they thought a child capable of doing, a fireman grumbled it would be better if she were kidnapped for "she would freeze in this weather." The forecast was for temperatures in the low forties, with a chance of showers, conditions that might leave a lightly clad little girl in a state of shock or worse.[23]

For the moment, the flippant suggestion about kidnapping was ignored by Mickey McCann, who took over the investigation. He saw no reason further to worry the Griffithses, who were becoming increasingly distressed by the more extreme views expressed on the street. Dave and Marion Griffiths recall that McCann was very gentle in his questions to them. He recapitulated the afternoon with them, borrowed a picture of the little girl, and promised that she would be returned unharmed. Then McCann issued a series of sharp, perfunctory orders. Some of the crowd were dispatched to search neighborhood basements and the partially constructed new homes again. Police Chief San Jule and his men agreed to check out the residences of carpenters and other workmen who had been at the building sites that day. In the meantime, the rest of the men—two or three hundred, the *Massena Observer* reported (Dave Griffiths puts the number at more than five hundred)— headed back into the woods with the troopers.

"It was thought that every foot of ground in the woods and elsewhere in the vicinity had been so thoroughly searched that there could be no possibility of overlooking the child." [24] Precious daylight moments were slipping away, and a search that had to be conducted in the dark might have an opposite affect from that intended. The sight of torches and flashlights flickering in the trees might so terrify a little girl that she would flee her rescuers. The use of dogs was rejected for basically the same reason. Eventually the men who went into the woods shoulder to shoulder would have to turn to flashlights, would establish little campsites with bonfires for the weary to warm themselves. But no dogs were ever used, and that was a mistake.

A grim Dave Griffiths, in mackinaw and hip boots, headed out again with McCann, George Ure, and the other men. Marion Griffiths went upstairs to stay with Mrs. Ure. There she was examined by her family doctor, Ralph MacAloon, who expressed concern for her mental state and the welfare of her as yet unborn child. MacAloon ordered her to keep away from the curious and well-meaning who still choked the Griffiths residence, inside and out. The only exceptions were Roy and Maude Contryman, friends of the Griffithses from the Grove District, both of whom were nurses, and who received permission to look after Marion Griffiths. Bobby Griffiths was sent to spend the night with Dorothy Taylor, whose husband had joined the search party. It was hoped she might take the boy's mind off what was happening, but Marion Griffiths concedes he must have known and worried.

There was no sleep or favorable news for Marion Griffiths that entire night. With darkness, frustration mounted, and those men who are always the first to volunteer assistance in crises and also the first to rationalize why they cannot stay to see the task through gave up the search. Others stayed in the fields through that chilly night, crisscrossing what seemed to be every foot of ground in a ten-mile-square region. South and east toward the area of the old springs, then west across Andres and down to the banks of the Grasse River, then south again to the town border with Louisville Township. In fog and a nippy drizzle that ate through their jackets. They trickled back in for coffee which neighbor women kept perking on the stove in the Griffiths apartment. Then they went out to look again.

Shortly after midnight, George Ure returned, his clothes muddied to the waist. Four hours later, a thoroughly exhausted Dave Griffiths staggered back from nine hours of scouring swamp and brush. Most of the time he had been alone with his thoughts and self-reproaches. Tearfully, Griffiths pleaded with the people manning the home base to let him go out again, but finally he was talked into lying down for a while on his living-room couch. Reluctantly, he agreed, but only on the condition that he be wakened by dawn or 6:00 A.M. at the very latest. The women let him rest until 8:00 A.M., when, somewhat perturbed at their good intentions, he rejoined the search. Griffiths and his wife were unaware that the focus of the affair had shifted away from the Nightingale Section during the night.

Governor Al Smith of New York. Campaign photo of 1928. "If bigotry and intolerance ... are going to succeed, it is dangerous for the future of the Republic, and the best way to kill anything un-American is to drag it out into the open." *(Courtesy of the private collection of Fred Chittock)*

Main Street of Massena, New York, 1928, looking in the direction of White's Hotel, right rear. *(Courtesy of the Massena Town Historical Society)*

Photo by

Another view of downtown Massena. The town then was pervaded by "a sneaky anti-Semitism, not the open kind. . . . There were all kinds of snide remarks made in groups behind people's backs," recalls the former Town Historian. *(Courtesy of the Massena Town Historical Society)*

Dave Griffiths, his son Bobby, and Barbara (circa 1927-1928). Barbara went into the woods to fetch her brother. *(Courtesy of Dave and Marion Griffiths)*

"Barbs" with doll at 8 Cherry Street, 1928. "There were some
wild animals out there—skunk, porcupines, deer, and a few
non-poisonous snakes—but nothing to worry about." *(Courtesy of Dave and Marion Griffiths)*

Massena firehouse and truck. Not a few of the 25–30 volunteers in 1928 were members of the Ku Klux Klan. *(Courtesy of the Massena Town Historical Society)*

Jake Shulkin and his son Willie before the storefront of Slavin & Shulkin's. "Willie had free run of the town . . . He wasn't dangerous. The police knew us. If there was any trouble, they'd just bring him home."—Mimi Shulkin Klein *(Courtesy of Mimi Shulkin Klein)*

4

*A*t 8:00 P.M. that Saturday evening, Jacob Shulkin was in his store on Water Street near the Main
Street Bridge. In those days, all the little shops in Massena Center stayed open late, until 9:00, on Saturdays.
This particular weekend, the Jewish shopkeepers had an
additional motive for keeping open. Sunday night
would mark the beginning of Yom Kippur, the Day of
Atonement. Tomorrow, all Jews in Massena would congregate at Adath Israel for the intonation of *Kol Nidre,*
the renunciation of false vows which might be taken in
the upcoming year. This would begin a twenty-four-
hour period of meditation, prayer, and abstinence. Instead of business as usual, Monday would see all Jewish
shops closed, all Jewish children in synagogue, not in
school, on this most sacred of Jewish holy days. Among
those certain to be at the synagogue throughout the

prayers was the congregation's president Jacob Shulkin.

Unlike his business partner, Sam Slavin (a brusque, portly man with dark, wavy hair and a face that was a cross between Ted Kennedy and Wendell Willkie), Jake Shulkin resembled not so much a political idol as he did a gnome. Balding, with wisps of fading hair about the peaked ears of a pixie and with a scalp speckled with the brown spots of age, Shulkin was a husky little man whose bent shoulders and large, loose-hanging hands gave him the appearance of being much shorter than his five feet nine inches.

Born in Belorussia in 1881, the year marking the beginning of the great time of troubles for Jews under the Romanovs, Jake had emigrated to the United States in 1902. His was a story all too familiar among the Jews of Eastern Europe. Lack of educational opportunity beyond three primary grades, a father who remarried, and a son who was now considered an outcast stepson in his own home. Discrimination at the hands of bigoted tsarist officials and ignorant, superstitious peasants, street brawls, and fear of the Damoclean pogrom and/ or expulsion. Faced with the prospect of fifteen years' military duty for a fatherland that despised him, Jake Shulkin emigrated 5,000 miles to America.[1]

For ten years, he labored in the sweatshops and pushed a peddler's cart in New York City. In 1906, Jake married his cousin, Sarah Seidel, a quiet woman one year his junior, who had emigrated from Warsaw. The following year, the first of their five children, William, or Willie, was born. While in New York, Shulkin met up with Sam Slavin, another recent arrival from the tsarist Pale. Somehow the two men scraped together a little cash in the hope of striking out from Manhattan's ghetto. First, they contacted one of Sarah's close relations, who operated a furniture store in upstate Gouverneur, New York. Then, in 1913, they opened Shulkin's and Slavin's in Massena, a sixty-foot-wide store where by 1928 one could purchase all kinds of major appliances—in later years, a new, all-electric Crosley showbox, an eight-tube electric neutrodyne radio, the finest Maytag wringer washers, the Steward Super Heater, "guaranteed to keep seven rooms at seventy degrees through the coldest winter months"—or even contract for a year's supply of propane bottled gas.[2]

Business was very good, and by 1927 the two men were able to open a second outlet, Majestic Furniture, 200 miles downstate in Rome, New York. Sam Slavin moved his wife and two children into a huge new gray frame house with green shutters on Bridges Street. Minnie Slavin, a spry, lovable little woman with a protective attitude toward the Jewish community of Massena, continues to live in the house after fifty years, fourteen years after her husband (whose oil portrait hangs on the wall of the parlor) died. The house, with its unique twin dining rooms, specially tiled country kitchen, bath with imported Dutch tile, three bedrooms of heavy oak furniture, red and purple Oriental rugs, tapestries, Dresden china, figurines, vases, and Westminster chimes, is a testimony to the prosperity enjoyed by the Slavins in that earlier period.

The Shulkin residence at 25 Maple Street was not

quite so impressive. Already forty years old when the family occupied it during World War I, the narrow, two-story building was located in a less desirable setting than that of the Slavins. From the upstairs bedrooms, one could look out on heavily traveled Route 37, the Main Street Bridge (only three doors away), or the town's two largest cemeteries (only 150 yards in either direction). The rear of the lot sloped abruptly to the Grasse River with its "healing" sulfur waters, which the Shulkin children were required to drink. Like most homes in Massena, the house had a low-slung front porch, with a rail consisting of spindle poles, and the inevitable Ionic columns favored in the Victorian Age. There were ten rooms, including two with bay windows on the first floor. These windows illuminated a double parlor, cluttered with a strange assortment of furniture— a daybed, two Windsor chairs and matching sofa, and an ornate eighteenth-century Cogswell chair with cabriole legs. According to Dora Shulkin Cohen, "My father was in the furniture business. At first, we had all the junk he took in trade. When he was more secure, we had more out of the stores, but nothing outstanding. My mother never even had good china. Just *milchik* and *fleischik* [dishes used in kosher homes for dairy or meat products]" [3]

Despite the usual social problems encountered by Jewish boys and girls in small towns (there were fights when the kids were called "Christ-killers" and little dating between Jews and Gentiles), and despite medical problems with sons Willie and Harold, the Shulkins' fifteen years in Massena were relatively happy ones. Jake was widely respected in the community. Marie

Elden-Brown recalled, "He was so good, so wonderful. 'How's your Red Cross funding coming?' he would ask. 'If you have any difficulty toward the end, come and see us.' And then all he would say was, 'How much do you need?' " [4] Successful businessman, bail bondsman, synagogue president, principal contributor to the Red Cross, eventually president of the Chamber of Commerce, Jake Shulkin was the model self-made man. During the World War I, he taught himself how to drive an automobile, and thereafter the family was never without one. The top-heavy, seven-passenger Studebaker that he drove regularly back and forth to Rome, the lush new cashmere coats that the boys received each winter, were evidence of the Shulkins' prosperity.

Jake's home was a meeting place for friends and relatives from Potsdam, Canton, and Ogdensburg. His wife was a *balabosta,* a woman who could make even a stranger feel welcome by quickly filling a table with the kind of kosher foods that left one's abdomen aflame with spices.[5] Sarah Shulkin was a frail woman, to whom thrift, moderation and cleanliness were the highest goods. She maintained coops for thirty or forty chickens out back, grew her own vegetables, and kept her home spotless. Her friend Minnie Slavin recalls her as "a sickly woman, but you should have seen how she kept that house. It was immaculate." [6]

Mrs. Shulkin reacted quietly to pressure and never disputed a word spoken by her husband. Her children do not recall her ever arguing openly with their father. "Maybe in private they argued," says her son Ben. "In those days, women had the vote and not much more." [7]

It could be questioned whether Sarah Shulkin had even that much. Her daughter Dora recalls, "When women got the vote, she voted the way my father voted." [8] And at that time, in the 1920s, everyone in Massena, including the Jews, voted Republican. Franklin Roosevelt had not yet displaced Abraham Lincoln as the idol of hyphenate Americans. Thus it was ironic that Jake Shulkin and his wife, who would soon require the assistance of Governor Al Smith, had never voted for Smith.

In the evening, the Shulkins would sit in the parlor or kitchen, listening to the radio. If she was not mending clothes or ironing, Sarah would stew a chicken in life-giving broth on the kitchen stove. Jake read *Der Tog,* the Yiddish daily newspaper from New York, relaying aloud the most striking news to her. Bad news everywhere, he would say. *"mir hobn zu zingen un zu zogn."* (We have no end of trouble.) Twenty thousand anti-Semitic acts in Germany alone in 1928. A *numerus clausus* at the University of Budapest, barring all Jewish students. Thirty-two Jews injured in a pogrom at Mohilev in the USSR; another 20 hospitalized in a disturbance at Wolkowishki, Lithuania. Another pogrom at Lemberg in Galicia that June; and they said that one was led by the Catholic priests. Although Jews constituted less than 10 percent of the population of Pilsudski's Poland, 891 of the 1,680 persons who committed suicide in that country that year were Jewish. Trouble in Rumania over Jews failing to abide by Sunday closing ordinances. A riot at the Wailing Wall in Jerusalem when Jews tried to set up stools for the aged during religious services. The chief Muslim official in Palestine, Haj Amin el-Husseini, the Grand Mufti of Jerusalem, was responsible for that. Two dozen persons had been hurt, and he threatened more incidents. The British did nothing. A Christian clergyman in Australia warned that Judaism was a precursor of agnosticism and that it was the greatest enemy of the Christian Church. No more Jews should be admitted to that land, which already was inundated with 5,000 adherents of the "Mosaic" faith.

The lunacy had even spread to the United States. Only a few weeks back, an Orthodox cemetery in Cleveland had been desecrated. Down in Bryant County, Georgia, the rednecks were trying to bar Jews from serving on any grand or petit juries. There was even talk of producing the vicious anti-Jewish Freiburg Passion Play in New York City the next spring. And the state of Connecticut was seriously considering outlawing *shehitah,* the ritual slaughter of animals, a rite essential to obtaining kosher meat.[9]

Jake Shulkin read how the ugly contagion of Judeophobia had spread over five continents like the scourge of smallpox. And as he read he consoled himself that at least it wasn't as bad in America as it was in Europe. It could never be that bad here. Certainly, some crazy people made noise or knocked over headstones, but never a pogrom. The American people did not know the meaning of the word, would never tolerate it. They weren't like the masses of ignorant Ukrainians or Croatians who suckled anti-Semitism with their mother's milk. Would you believe, Jake would find himself shouting angrily at his wife, there had been a revival of the ritual-murder charge in Europe that year! The *goyim* in Zaklikow, Poland; Petrovo Selo, Yugoslavia; Cologne, Germany—all had been excited by the canard that Jews were killing Gentiles for secret religious rites that fall. And, oh yes, there had been one earlier attempt to slander the Jews in this manner, at Easter, April 1928, in Salonika, Greece.[10] Jake Shulkin, a man unafraid of the Ku Klux Klan, always shook his head when he read such things. *"Dos ken nit aher passieren,"* he told his wife, (That can't happen here.)

This Saturday evening, Jake Shulkin was at the little roll-top desk in the rear of his store, going over accounts. Normally his daughter Dora, a plump, myopic girl of fifteen would handle these, but things had been somewhat chaotic during the High Holy Days. Because business seemed even more slack than usual, Sam Slavin had gone home early. Only Jake and his son Willie, moving stock items, sweeping, trying to look busy, were in the store.

For the Shulkins, twenty-two-year-old Willie was at once their *hatzlachah* and *kalalah* (blessing and curse). Their first born, this sad-eyed young man with the wild shock of hair brushed back like a lion's mane, had never given them much trouble while growing up. Not especially bright, he had gone through grade school with average marks. Like his siblings, he attended heder (religious school) "because Dad said, 'Go.'" [11] The Shulkin children and other Jewish children in Massena sat about Rabbi Berel Brennglass, learning Hebrew phonetically. Those who did well were rewarded with pieces of rock candy. Comedians or laggards were boxed on the ear. "The truth is," says Mimi Shulkin Klein, "it was so bad we never learned anything." [12] Willie did master his required *Haftorah* portion for his bar mitzvah at the age of thirteen. Then he delivered a speech ghostwritten for him by Rabbi Brennglass and was presented, like all Jewish boys of a bygone era, with an Eversharp fountain pen as an acknowledgment of his manhood. That his behavior was already somewhat peculiar was excused by Jake and Sarah Shulkin, who said, *"Willie iz nokh a yung yingl."* (Willie is still a young boy.)

The boy's behavior never improved. No one is quite certain how to explain it. It may have had something to do with the onset of puberty or Willie's social retardation. Never close to his brothers or sisters, he had, Ben states, "no friends." Some Massenans suggest that the problem was genetic, that Jake and Sarah, being first cousins, ran the Mendelian chance of having recessive traits emerge in their offspring.[13] People still recall how Harold, the youngest of the Shulkins' five children, embarrassed the family in 1923 when, at the age of eight, he wandered into a church one Sunday and disrupted the service by announcing to the dumbfounded congregants that he was having visions and revelations. Always a sickly, nervous child, Harold died quite young, in his early thirties.[14]

About the time Harold began acting up, Willie's problems also became more acute. What earlier had been excused as the normal tantrums of an adolescent now appeared to be classic symptoms of hypomania. Brother Ben says flatly, "He was a manic-depressive.

When he was 'up,' he was extremely active. He would start to talk and never shut up." [15] Willie's sisters Dora and Mimi concur, adding, "His tongue would go off in all directions." [16] He would belabor people on the street: "Do you know why I did that? Why I said that? I don't know. Nobody knows. Nobody knows anything." [17] During such periods (which might last for weeks or months), Willie was quick to anger, sloppy about his personal appearance. He would quote from books he once read and try unsuccessfully to make puns, jokes, or rhymes. "What do you know about the Silver [sic] War?" he once asked Mimi. "You never shot a gun." [18] He made mistakes in identity, greeting strangers as old friends, sometimes creating a nuisance in the store.

People seeing Willie in his "up" state, gesturing wildly, laughing or frowning without reason, talking to himself in spurts, might tend to agree with the former editor of the town's paper that he was "crazy." [19] The president of Massena's Chamber of Commerce claimed "he had a tendency to violence." [20] Another Jewish merchant would regard him with disgust as "that kid with a sixteen IQ." [21] Somewhat harshly, his brother Ben would say, "Willie wasn't playing with a full deck." [22] Sister Dora more benignly stated, "He was never sick. He just wasn't very bright." [23] For the Jewish community generally, he was an embarrassment, a *chelemer,* the proverbial fool.

It was impossible for Willie to continue in school. For a while, the Shulkins tried to divert some of his energies by giving him work in the store. His father taught him to drive the car and delivery truck, and permitted him to run errands about town. Willie also delivered some of the bottled gas that Shulkin and Slavin's supplied to the townsfolk. The work did little to temper his condition, and Willie's behavior threatened to cost the two merchants some of their business.

Finally, Jake and Sarah Shulkin agreed to hospitalize their son. He was admitted to Ogdensburg State Hospital, a brooding complex of antiquated wood-and-brick buildings, an hour down the road from Massena. Again, no one knows what went on behind the wire windows because such information is privileged. Ben Shulkin maintains that his brother must have undergone electroshock therapy while in Ogdensburg because "when he got out, they had knocked out what intelligence he had." [24] In fact, shock therapy was not introduced to the United States until 1940, two years after it was first used in Italy,[25] more than a decade after the incident at Massena.

Perhaps the doctors at Ogdensburg felt Willie's case was not so severe, that cold wet packs applied in bed would suffice to calm him. Perhaps they made use of hydrotherapy, placing him without restraints in a tub for several hours, or with straps and hooks in the continuous flow bath for as much as four days. Medicine in the 1920s knew little of tranquilizers, even less of the long-range effects of barbituric acid derivatives, trional and paraldehyde in cases of hypomania. And there was metrazol shock, ampules of coramine adrenalin chloride, 4 cubic centimeters of 10 percent solution, injected intravenously. Within thirty seconds, the patient's eyelids would quiver. His face would pale, and he would feel as if he were going to die. With loss of consciousness came convulsions. Nurses were required to hold the patient's shoulder and pelvis on the bed, and a gag was inserted in the mouth to prevent dislocation of the lower jaw. To prevent fractures of other bones and to control the convulsions, 20 milligrams of intocostrin, a form of the poison curare, would then be injected into the bloodstream. Finally, the patient would collapse into a brief, comatose sleep. When he awoke, confused, incontinent, he would be given 7½ grains of sodium amytal to induce a relaxed sleep. Most patients improved, we are told, "after three or four treatments." [26] One can only speculate what impact such "treatment" may have had upon Willie Shulkin, alone and frightened behind the sterile gray walls of Ogdensburg.

Because it was clear the hospital was having little positive effect upon Willie, despite some financial outlay by the Shulkins, the boy was withdrawn and brought home. There seemed every likelihood that he would readjust more quickly if he were free. A survey of 8,000 manic-depressives released from New York State hospitals between 1909 and 1930 indicated that fewer than half were readmitted.[27] More significantly, Judaism offers no justification for the shutting away of those who are not deemed dangerous. An individual who may seem irresponsible or "muddleheaded," yet is generally lucid, is absolved from religious or legal obligations. Society is bound to protect, not detain, him, just as it would protect the deaf-and-mute or a minor.[28]

After his stay in the hospital, Willie possessed little

memory. He looked and talked like an adult, but in his judgment he was little more than a child. His mind was naive and innocent, extremely impressionable, grasping only the most colorful images of his world. He knew he was Jewish, and he knew that being Jewish was to be even more different than he already was. He remembered the awful things Rabbi Brennglass and Eli Friedman had taught them in the Young Judea meetings of Jewish suffering in the *Galut* (exile). The burnings, rapes, and expulsions had been reinforced by his father's nightly discourses while reading *Der Tog*. Death was an everyday occurrence in his life as he watched funeral processions along Maple Street.

Unlike many parents who in that period of insensitivity "hid" their emotionally disturbed children, the Shulkins determined to restore an element of normality to Willie's existence. He went back to work in the store, was given his old duties, and was permitted to function as autonomously as possible. It was as if Willie understood. He tried desperately to please—not just his parents but everyone in town. At times he was unobtrusive, his head down, as if in intense meditation. At other times he was like a child, open, friendly, but not clutching. No one showed much concern for "Young Willie" or "the Shulkin boy" anymore.

Jake Shulkin looked up from his books and regarded his son with love and pain. If Ben looked in the mirror each morning and saw his father, Willie was a double for his beloved Sarah. No matter what anyone said of the boy, for Jake, Willie was a *lamedvovnik,* one of the thirty-six Just Men set on earth by the Lord to take upon their shoulders the suffering of mankind without any reward.

"Go on home, Willie," Jake said tenderly. "I don't think there's much more for you to do here."

Willie smiled. "Okay, Papa."

He set down the broom he was pushing across the floor of the store and walked to the open door. He paused for a moment, waved, then went out. He didn't go home.

5

The historian Lee M. Friedman has tried to explain what happened in Massena later that Saturday evening in 1928. According to Friedman's account, a rumor spread through town "like wildfire" that Barbara Griffiths had been murdered by Jews who needed her blood for rites connected with the upcoming Yom Kippur holy day. The tales grew wilder as people heard how "two, three children's bodies had been found!" Friedman refers to "the Jew tailor" who had been seen with "a suspicious pair of shears." "The Jewish doctor" had bought some ether. The local expressman had just the previous day delivered a large case "big as a coffin" to the "Massena Emporium" which "the little Jew ran." As people congregated at street corners, they fretted, "Perhaps the Jews would murder them all!" [1]

The source of such gossip:

> The old Polish farmer from that queer hovel on the old West Road was overheard repeating the story

told him years ago in the old country by his mother's grandmother that when she was a little girl, in the village where she was born, one Easter all the Jews from the countryside foregathered in the village and in the night-time murdered a little lad—the son of the village baker—and then they went to their synagogue and drank his blood from a ram's horn and went mad, shouting strange words of black magic. From the grave at the edge of the forest in which they had hidden the body a voice kept crying: "Oh, Mother of God! Rescue me, a poor murdered child!" until the villagers dug up the body and gave it a Christian burial. Then the people fell upon the Jews and drove them from the village. What a lot of fine clothing and jewels they left behind! Enough to give every girl a dress and a gem and "my dear great-grandmother showed me the ring she had, to prove it was all true." [2]

Unfortunately, Friedman, who published his detailed account, *Pilgrims in a New Land,* for the prestigious Jewish Publication Society of America, was in error. There was a sizable Polish population in the Grove District of Massena, and at least one source agrees the Poles brought their prejudices with them from the old country. ("What people do not know, they fear.") [3] There was even a Jewish tailor (Ben Cohen), but according to eighty-four-year-old Eli Friedman (dean of Massena's Jewish community), he never acted suspiciously and "rarely poked his head, let alone his shears, outside his store." Friedman and another Massena old-timer, Jack Jacobs, agree there was no Jewish doctor, no Massena Emporium. After both men finished laughing at Friedman's account ("Isn't that some writing? The whole thing is a piece of fiction cut out of whole cloth"), they also agreed that there was no "old Polish farmer." [4] Even the most reticent townsfolk agree that the fatal catalyst was supplied by another foreigner—a Greek.

Albert Comnas operated the Crystal Palace, the ice-cream parlor and café in the Central Building at Andrews and Main. It was a modest little place with an unimaginative decor—pale-green walls and a checkered tile floor, a few booths and tables, and a counter where Comnas, a recent immigrant to Massena, served coffee as well as sodas. A short, burly, clean-shaven man, Comnas was eager to please the people in his newly adopted home, eager to pass with old-timers who found the location of his shop convenient and the Greek amusing, if somewhat coarse. As he struggled for acceptance and financial solvency, Comnas muttered curses about his countryman and neighbor, John Pilialoglous. [5]

Like Comnas, Pilialoglous had been born in Macedonia shortly before the turn of the century. He emigrated to the United States in 1914, coming first to work as a waiter in Miami Beach, then moving to a more familiar northern clime. From the money he saved working in a cheese factory in Ogdensburg, he was able to start a restaurant, the Boston Lunch Restaurant on Main Street. Later, he was to own a second place, the Silver Grill on Orvis Street, and to cater the dining room of White's, the only hotel in Massena. Life was very rewarding for John Pilialoglous, his wife, Margaret, and their several children. They lived in a large Victorian house on Andrews Avenue, directly across from the home of Mayor W. Gilbert Hawes. Though his wife could barely communicate in English, Pilialoglous was quite popular in town. Several hundred persons turned out to his wedding feast, celebrated above a downtown drugstore in 1924. The balding Greek with the flat head and serious look was also considered a "great friend" and "a liberal" by Massena's Jews, who were among his best customers and with whom he regularly played pinochle.[6]

Living in a single rented room, unmarried, Comnas bitterly envied Pilialoglous. An incident that occurred some years later demonstrates his contempt for the company Pilialoglous kept. By that time, Comnas had married (a local girl who was a telephone operator), and the union had produced a son. One day, when the boy was in the shop with his father, Saul Rosenbaum entered to grab a cup of coffee. Comnas took his son's shoulders and pointed him around, saying excitedly, "See! See! That man. It's a Jew." [7] Comnas's bias against Jews was well known, and Massena's Jews used to say that the death of his son at an early age was punishment for the father's hatreds.[8]

Albert Comnas required no education when it came to the Jews. In his hometown of Salonika, 75,000 of the 120,000 residents were Jewish. And while Jews had lived in the region at least since the time of Saint Paul, they were still considered foreigners. In the great national uprising of 1821–1829, Jewish communities at Agrinion, Patras, Tripolitsa, Mistra, Thebes, and Livadia had been all but extirpated. Before the Balkan Wars and World War I shuffled boundaries and nationalities, there were only 9,000 Jews in Greece proper, loosely distributed among Corfu, Larissa, Chalcis, Trikkala, Arta, and Athens. Only the centuries of protection afforded them by the Ottoman sultans permitted the Jews of Macedonia to flourish.[9]

For Comnas, the Jewish Hospital and B'nai B'rith lodge, the Jewish schools, handicraft and silk shops, shipping and banking firms in Salonika all were affronts, symbols of the subjugation of his people by the hated Turks and their exploiting allies, the Jews. While most Macedonian Jews hovered at the brink of starvation, all he could see were the bankers, physicians, and lawyers who helped underwrite the Committee of Union and Progress and the Young Turk Revolution of 1908. For Comnas, the thirty-seven synagogues that dotted Salonika were exactly what Saint John Chrysostom had said of Jewish houses of worship: "worse than a brothel . . . the den of scoundrels and the repair of wild beasts . . . the temple of demons devoted to idolatrous cults . . . the refuge of brigands and debauchees, and the cavern of devils . . . a criminal assembly . . . a place of meeting for the assassins of Christ . . . a den of thieves, a house of ill fame, a dwelling of iniquity, the refuge of devils, a gulf and abyss of perdition." [10]

Comnas was a devout member of the Greek Orthodox Church, and he wholly subscribed to the views espoused by the fourth-century Archbishop of Constantinople, the leading sage of the Byzantine rite. How often in the course of educating small children had the priests made use of the homilies of this man whom Cardinal Newman had called "a bright, cheerful, gentle soul, a sensitive heart, a temperament open to emotion and impulse; and all this elevated, refined, transformed by a touch of heaven—such was St. John Chrysostom." [11] Comnas grew up listening to and being indoctrinated with the dictates of Saint John that Jewish misery and homelessness were part of divine vengeance for their wrongful interpretations of Scripture, for their assassination of His Son, because God hated the Jews. How could one develop compassion for a people whose debauchery, greed, and treachery had brought them to the level of the goat or pig? As Saint John had taught: "They know only one thing, to satisfy their stomachs, to get drunk, to kill and beat each other up like stage villains and coachmen." [12]

Comnas knew that the Jews were not merely avaricious bloodsuckers eager to cheat the Gentile, just as their Talmud commanded. It was a documented fact that throughout history the Jews had been regarded as the principal spreaders of disease. Typhus, typhoid, diphtheria, leprosy, cholera, syphilis, it didn't matter. They were blamed for the Great Plague of 1348–1350 when 40,000,000 people from Strasbourg to Salonika died of typhus. People said the Jews accomplished this by selling tainted meat (upon which their children had previously urinated) to Christians. Or the Jews ground up the entrails and hearts of cadavers along with frogs' legs, snakes' heads, spiders, lizards, and "the drool of a red-headed woman buried alive" to make a powder that could be spread on the ground, placed in wells, or somehow used to poison the air. Such tales had to be true, else why would thousands of them have been tortured, broken on the wheel, forcibly baptized and drowned, or burned at the stake in Switzerland, Bavaria, Savoy, and Swabia? [13]

Even worse, the Jews allegedly ridiculed the sacred rite of transubstantiation. Since the twelfth century,

there had been more than a hundred incidents in which
it was charged that a group of misanthropic rabbans
(masters), determined to impose suffering anew upon
Christ, somehow ferreted a Host out of a church. Then,
having chanted some magical formula, these evil crea-
tures gleefully stabbed the wafer and watched either the
form of a child appear or blood flow from it. The
perpetrators of this foul deed invariably were struck
dumb or blind. And subsequently the rest of the Jewish
community was made to pay for their miscreance in
blood. After one such charge in Franconia in 1298,
50,000 Jews were slaughtered.[14] The amazing thing was
that with so much emphasis on the stealth and furtive-
ness of the plotters, no *pogromchik* ever paused to wonder how it was that the Jews were always found out.

The canard against the Jews that gained most promi-
nence in Europe, however, was that of ritual murder.
Every year, it was believed, a sinister body of Zionist
elders met somewhere to recreate the passion of Christ
at Easter. For their purposes, they required a young
Christian child, an innocent whose blood, like that of
Christ, would be pure. Such a child would be kidnapped, fattened up like a paschal lamb, then sacrificed
in a ceremony closely following the crucifixion of Jesus.
A crown of thorns supposedly would be placed on the
child's head, and he would be beaten. Then he would
be "slaughtered," "ritually," with the goal of drawing
off his blood, which apparently possessed magical qualities. The Jews needed this blood, their detractors said,
to heal the circumcision wound, or because Jewish *men*
lost blood through menstruation, or because all Jewish
children were born blind and only Gentile blood could

cure them, or to cover the garlic-sweet *foetor Judaicus,* the "Jew stench" that every Jew possessed.[15] Later it was maintained the Jews ground up the blood into their Purim cakes, or Hamantaschen. And, finally, it was decided that since the Jews were so merry at Passover (the festival commemorating their deliverance from bondage in Egypt), the blood had to be used to make their matzoth, the unleavened bread to which medieval Christians ascribed all kinds of magical qualities. The annual coincidence of Passover and Easter seemed to confirm the belief that the Jews intended to mock the sufferings of Christ.[16]

After the first such charge (in Kiev in 1096), whenever a Gentile child disappeared, it was pogrom season against the Jewish community. No one bothered to think how stupid it was of the Jews once more to make elaborate preparations, execute their plans, then dump the corpse of the martyred child into the nearest shed or stream where it could easily be recovered and where upon recovery its dead arms would twitch miraculously, pointing accusingly in the direction of the Jewish quarter. Nor could people bother with medical testimony like that of the Czech University of Prague during the Polna ritual-murder affair in 1899 that no blood had been taken from the victim's body.[17] In fact, people did not even require a victim to establish a claim of ritual murder against the Jews. In Toledo, Spain, in 1490, there was no proof that a victim even existed, yet five Jews were executed for the "crime," as "it was universally believed that God had completed the parallel between Christ and the Niño, and on the third day, had carried the body up to heaven." [18]

The child who wandered off and was never heard from again, the child whose body had been ravaged by wild animals, the child who had been molested by some medieval deviant, the child kidnapped and slain by brigands, the prodigal slain by an angered parent, the young girl raped by some overzealous suitor, all these brutalities and more were heaped at the door of the Jews. The Jews would be tortured, their property confiscated, their synagogues fired, and dozens burned at the stake, as in Blois, France, in 1171, again when no victim was produced.[19] Then a lucrative shrine in memory of the martyred Christian soul would be established. Indigents and cripples would come from all over Europe, slavering for the miracles that could be dispensed (at a cost) by local priests. Some of these child-saints were still working miracles into the nineteenth century.[20]

Traditionally, because of the contrast in mood between Easter and Passover, the ritual-murder charge was linked with the spring of the year. But for Gentiles ignorant of their own Mass and believing in the authenticity of enough splinters of the True Cross to make an ark for all the animals of the world, for people so gullible they lit candles before one of the three heads of John the Baptist or one of the three arms of Saint Peter on display in European churches, it mattered little whether it was Passover or *Tu b'Shevat,* the Jewish Arbor Day that comes in midwinter. All Jewish holidays sounded alike, and the disappearance of a Gentile youth around *Rosh Chodesh* (the monthly advent of the new moon) would have sufficed to justify the charge of ritual murder and its ensuing pogrom.

Frederick II, Innocent IV, and Gregory X had all

condemned the blood libel as early as the thirteenth century. Subsequent popes revoked beatification of the child-saints in the eighteenth century.[21] But papal decrees do not erase the fears and hatreds nurtured by fifty generations of men. Albert Comnas knew nothing of "official" positions on ritual murder. He was a simple man, a devout man, and he knew that there had to be some truth to the charge. How else to explain the fact that the Jews had been charged with ritual murder in Damascus and Rhodes in 1840, Marmora in 1843, Smyrna in 1864, and Corfu in 1891, not to mention his hometown of Salonika the previous spring? How else to explain the recent rash of charges at Tatar Pazardzhik, Bulgaria, in 1894; Bakau, Rumania, in 1892; Rzeszow, Galicia, in 1882; Ingrandes, France, in 1892; Nagyszokol, Hungary, in 1891; Konitz, Prussia, in 1900; Xanten, in the Rhineland, in 1892; Kishinev, Bessarabia, in 1903; or Kiev in 1911? [22]

It was always the same. A young child found with his or her throat slashed by "the slaughterer's cut," his or her blood drained off (no matter what medical experts said, the blood had been drained off). Then a public spectacle where the accused—his name might be Adolf Burchhoff or Leopold Hilsner or Adolf Lewy or Mendel Beiliss, it didn't matter—the Jew—would be acquitted. Jewish money, international Jewish influence, that's what did it. The courts could be bought. Even the tsar of Russia, with his notorious disaffection for the Jews, might be bought. But the people couldn't be fooled. Just like the Beiliss trial in Russia. That big clod was exonerated, but the peasant jury affirmed that ritual murder had been done to little Andrei Yuschinsky.[23]

Comnas must have been ruminating over some of these thoughts that Saturday evening as he tended his customers. The town was all excited about the disappearance of the little girl. Nothing like this had ever happened here before. Interesting that the Jewish merchants in town weren't closing shop and running out to join the search. Tomorrow was a Jewish holiday, a big Jewish holiday, he vaguely understood.

For the thousandth time, Comnas mulled over that peculiar relationship of John Pilialoglous and the Jews. Pilialoglous came from the same region, had been taught the same ideas, was as devout as Comnas, perhaps even more so. The Pilialoglous home was a veritable Byzantine cathedral with its icons, pictures of saints and holy men, bric-a-brac, candelabra, Grecian vases. And yet Pilialoglous let those people come into his house, even played pinochle with them. Probably would not even object if his daughter married one.

What happened next is difficult to establish. The following is the best we can do to piece together a sequence of crucial events:

An old-timer, Eli Friedman, flatly blames Comnas for the origin of the ritual-murder libel in Massena. Friedman maintains that at least one of the state troopers involved in the search for Barbara Griffiths was dining at the Crystal Palace that evening. "The troopers weren't well paid," he told me. "Normally, though, they ate at Pilialoglous's. They didn't go into his [Comnas's] store. But these were new men. Comnas told them something: 'The Jews are having a holiday. Maybe they need blood.' " [24] This version is supported by statements of Saul Rosenbaum and Abe Kauffman, along with Lou Greenblatt's researches. In his interview with Jake Shulkin, Greenblatt learned that Comnas allegedly went out of his restaurant to tell the troopers of his suspicions concerning the Jews.[25]

For the most part, Jack Jacobs agrees. Only he expands the number of listeners to include members of Massena's volunteer fire department, the group notorious for its Klan sympathies. "It had to be a native European," Jacobs told me. "The Greek who ran the 'greasy spoon' on Main Street. The gang in the fire station would never have known about it. The native boys wouldn't have come up with the idea. It was *Erev* Yom Kippur. With the men in getting coffee and him serving, he may have said, 'In the old country, you see, Jews are known for this.' I don't think he meant anything by it. But a lot of ignorant people listened to him spout." [26]

At that moment, Willie Shulkin entered the ice-cream parlor.

Saul Rosenbaum: "He was on the street all the time. We were open late Saturday and Wednesday nights. He was there that night." [27]

Dora Cohen: "He was allowed to stay downtown. It was only a block away from home." [28]

Mimi Klein: "Of course, Willie had free run of the town. He was twenty-one or twenty-two. He wasn't dangerous. The police knew us. If there was any trouble, they'd just bring him home." [29]

Dora Cohen: "There wasn't much to do on Saturday nights in Massena. The Library was closed. He might have stopped in the restaurant for a soda or candy." [30]

72

Mimi Klein and Lou Greenblatt: "The Crystal Palace was a perfect place for Willie." [31]

Jack Jacobs: "He came as an adult into the restaurant. Someone asked Willie if he knew anything about the girl's disappearance." [32]

Ben Shulkin (snidely): "Willie knew from Sunday school about the ritual-murder libel. He said, 'I hope they don't blame this on the Jews.'" [33]

Jack Jacobs: "He may have done it subconsciously." [34]

Mimi Klein: "He easily may have made the comment. He probably saw it as an opportunity to get recognition." [35]

Whatever the case, the formula for trouble was nearly complete—a missing Gentile girl, the ritual-murder libel raised, the libel unsquelched by the first of what Harry Levine called "two loose-lipped Jews." [36] As the *New York Post* put it: "After all other efforts to find the child failed, the investigators began to work on the theory that possibly some person or persons had kidnaped the child and destroyed her. In starting on this theory, the first person to be investigated was the Jewish boy Jacob Shaulkin [sic]." [37]

6

Less than a block from Comnas's "greasy spoon" was Massena City Hall. This weathered brick building had housed the offices of village and town government for more than a century. Townsfolk were rather fond of the two-and-one-half-story gray structure with its "Doric portico supported by four large square white columns." [1] (Actually the six-foot-high columns are Corinthian, and the cupolated effect smacks not so much of an American house of government as it does a Byzantine church shrunk one tenth in scale.) Before extensive WPA remodeling in 1938–1939, the building also served as the cultural center of Massena, replete with a dance hall, opera house, and balcony on the second floor. Traveling vaudevillians delighted the residents of Saint Lawrence County here, and on not a few occasions some of these troupes were abandoned by mustache-tweaking managers who made off with the night's proceeds.[2]

City Hall has always held a peculiar magnetism for the people of Massena. Even today it is striking that while young people elsewhere may despise "pigs," Massena's youth may be found at all hours of the evening, and particularly on the weekends, clustered on the steps of the police station. It was so in 1928. All evening, people milled about the block at Main and Orvis streets, wandering in and out of the basement headquarters of the village police. Hopelessly inadequate, the police station consisted of two rooms for the patrolmen and Chief San Jule, plus several vermin-infested cells for derelicts.

With every passing moment, San Jule was increasingly thankful that he had not been saddled with the present difficult task. ("He would have stumbled if he had ever come across a clue," one detractor told me.) Instead, San Jule offered his facilities to Troopers McCann and Hughes as a command post. Poor McCann, already fatigued by his own reconnaissance of the Nightingale Section, frustrated by unsuccessful searches about town, and anxious to produce something to preserve the reputation of the service, was losing control of the situation. More and more, the crazy whispers—animals, Indians, kidnapping, drowning, maybe even a crazy man—were gaining acceptance as wearied searchers returned to mingle with the people standing about downtown. And now another rumor—that the Jews had taken the kid. Even Mayor Hawes seemed intrigued by that one.

W. Gilbert Hawes was an officious man whose trademark was an ever-present bow tie and whose greatest knack was that of being reelected village president, or mayor, of Massena. Since 1922, he had succeeded in that venture five times during the annual March elections. Good fortune seemed to have favored the quiet-spoken native of Tarrytown, New York, since his arrival in town during World War I to work at the Diamond Creamery. A tall, handsome man whose rough-hewn, jut-jawed head sat on a spiney neck, Hawes had married a lovely downstate woman of some means. Combining her resources with a crash course in pasteurization at Cornell, Hawes then opened his own dairy—H. and H. Dairy—and rapidly monopolized the supply of bottled milk for Massena.[3]

Unlike his partner, Frank Holiday, who preferred to live unpretentiously, Hawes was a restless man, another seeker after status in the community. His chance came in 1922 when the Democratic Party, a perpetual loser in Massena in those days, nominated him for mayor. His election that year must have surprised Hawes as much as it did everyone else in town. Old-timers rationalize this fluke, saying that there had been another Hawes family resident in town for a number of years, a popular family that ran a lumber business. People must have voted for W. Gilbert by mistake, I was told, thinking they were voting for the other Hawes.[4]

However he was elected, Hawes proved to be a fairly capable administrator. In seven years, he paved most of Massena's downtown streets (three and a half miles, he claimed), instituted semiweekly garbage collections, improved the water supply, and constructed new sewers, all while simultaneously cutting the tax rate from 15.45 mills to 14.50 and limiting indebtedness to an increase of $5,000.[5] He also converted to the Republican Party and moved from his old home on Clark Street to the Andrews House, Massena's landmark residence on the road bearing the same name. Nestled on a huge lot of maples and oaks, no more than 200 yards from downtown, Andrews House was the most sumptuous of homes in Massena. Built in 1831 from rough gray stone quarried from the bed of the Grasse River,[6] its many windows and arched doorways are striking to this day.

Ernest Wagar of the Chamber of Commerce recalls, "They were *the* people then." [7] There were frequent parties, with guests from Massena and surrounding communities arriving in limousines. There were regular treks to the nine-hole golf course out on Route 12 (since submerged by the Saint Lawrence Seaway). Hawes even constructed a skating rink in the rear of the house for use by neighbor children.

Indeed, it may be that Hawes's preoccupation with children (he had three of his own) prompted his interest in the disappearance of the Griffiths girl. Seward Hanmer, whose father served as head of the Board of Supervisors during Hawes's administration, suggests that Hawes may have been somewhat immature himself, as he derived "an inordinate pleasure" out of being with the young.[8] Certainly, by 1928, Hawes's marriage had begun to deteriorate. Both he and his wife were drinking heavily, despite Prohibition. And it would not be too many years before Mrs. Hawes would scandalize the town by running off with a dandy imported by the mayor to serve as secretary for Massena's Chamber of Commerce.[9] The mayor's obsession with doing things for children, therefore, may have been one way of bolstering a flagging ego.

Devout, Congregationalist like the Griffithses, ostentatious, insecure yet pompous, this was W. Gilbert Hawes. "A typical goy in the dairy business," says Dora Cohen.[10] "An idiot," says Jack Jacobs.[11] And when word buzzed through town on Saturday evening that the Jews might have had something to do with the disappearance of Barbara Griffiths, it was impulsive, gullible, poorly educated Hawes, likening himself to a shepherd tending his flock, who overrode the objections of a disbelieving Chief Floyd San Jule and belabored Trooper Mickey McCann to make an inquiry into the charge against the Jews.

"It was typical of people when they get excited," Seward Hanmer observes. "Some ignorant people started a rumor that there was an old religious celebration at that time of year. A ritual through the history of the Jewish people from biblical times. At this ceremony they would kill and eat anything as a sacrifice. A small child, for example. Somehow the rumor got out that the mayor said it. No one will know if he did or didn't." [12]

It was as if a cesspool of hate had suddenly been tapped, and now Neanderthal, carnivore, budding rapist, blood avenger, howler at the moon, *haidamak*, crusader all materialized in Massena. Things that of themselves should not have counted for much—the bias of a religious zealot, the ignorance of a backwoods politician, the braggadocio of a retarded boy—now struck like hammer blows at the walls of civilization.

Newspaper editor Leonard Prince admits, "It moved very fast. The town was very tight-knit, very excited." [13]

Saul Rosenbaum was preparing to lock up the doors of Stone & Co. Ready to Wear Clothing, which he operated with Joseph Stone and Stone's brother-in-law Eli Friedman on Main Street just north of Andrews. Rosenbaum had come to Massena from his birthplace of Grodno, Lithuania, in 1924. Like practically all the Jewish businessmen in town, he was diminuitive, no more than five feet five inches tall. A wispish man, his image of harmlessness is accentuated by soft, sad eyes that ever seem on the verge of tears. If the reader can imagine a Jewish Barry Jones, the distraught atomic scientist of *Seven Days to Noon,* he has a picture of Saul Rosenbaum.

Rosenbaum was not, however, a man to be regarded lightly. A dedicated pacifist ("Vietnam and Kent State are two crimes for which no one has yet been punished," he says), he would frequently dispute Scripture with his Gentile neighbors. For him, Jesus Christ was a figure who legitimately belonged within the province of Judaism. The Jesus whom Christians adored was but an invention of Greek and pagan theology. "Christians have no more genuine claim to Jesus's teachings than they do to those of Buddha," he would say gruffly. "Where do they practice 'the meek shall inherit the earth' or 'love thy enemy'? What law has been fulfilled by their interpretations of his teachings? The more you read about Christianity, the less you know it has to do with Jesus. Most people who are Christians must know that, but they're just blank followers." [14]

With such candor, it should not surprise that one of the first places searched when McCann and Hawes gave their blessing to a hunt was Stone & Co. There were only a few clerks standing by when "two or three fellows from the fire station" entered the store. One of them was Roy Countryman. Rosenbaum does not remember the other two. They were the faceless men of a pogrom.

"They wanted to search the place," says Rosenbaum. "I imagine they had been out looking for the girl. 'Maybe she went down in your cellar,' they said. I said, 'I didn't see any child.' The only way into the basement was through the front door of the store. There were no doors or windows downstairs. They demanded to see the basement. There were two or three of them, and they were bigger than I was. I didn't like it, but I didn't say anything more. They went downstairs. All they found was just men's clothing in boxes. Then they left." [15]

The only thing that prevented similar scenes from being enacted at Kauffman's or Shulkin and Slavin's was that the owners of these places had already locked up and gone home. Nonetheless, the glare of flashlights danced across cellar walls and storeroom boxes that night, and the vigilantes would return to peer into the same windows the next morning, as if by chance they might catch the Jews at some unholy rite.

"Craziest excitement you've ever seen." Cole Cummins commented. "People running all over town, with no rhyme, no reason." In his ninety-three years in Massena, forty-three of them as clerk and paymaster at Alcoa, through the Depression and even after Pearl

Harbor, Cummins never witnessed such hysteria in town. A lanky, shy bachelor with the tragic habit of the lonely for record-keeping, Cummins lived alone in a rooming house only a few doors down from the Shulkins on Maple Street. He knew Jake Shulkin ("an honorable man") and his son Willie ("not normal, but harmless"), and was sympathetic toward their problem ("all towns have people like that"). Cole Cummins's grandparents had encountered hostility against Irish Catholics when they emigrated to America during the Know Nothing mania of the 1850s, but neither Cole nor his brother Bob had known any real prejudice while growing up on the family farm in nearby Raymondville. Both were liked and respected, and Bob was now serving in the Hawes administration as village Water Commissioner.

Cummins had put in a full day at the plant across the river and missed the initial excitement caused by Barbara Griffiths's disappearance. So also had he missed the great search mounted in the twilight. Only now, late in the evening, as he walked into town, as he always did on Saturdays in search of companionship, was he apprised of the situation.

"I met a man, a man I've known all my life, out on Main Street," Cummins told me. "He was one of the fire station crowd. A Kluxer. He asked me, 'Didn't you ever hear about them people and their sacrifices?' I told him, 'I've lived here all my life and never heard of it. Always been Jewish people here, and they've never molested anyone. Why, the Kauffmans have been here practically since the town started. This thing's a lie for thousands of years. How do you know it's true? What proof do you have?"

THE INCIDENT AT MASSENA

"You know what they did? What they said?" asked Cummins. "They thought I was simple." [16]

"We lived downtown, but I don't remember the mobs. There was just a grim quiet." These are the recollections of Eleanor Dumas, recently editor of a bicentennial history of Massena. "My mother [Ella Lahey] was a good friend of the Griffiths. She went to their house to see what she could do, bring food, help out. Our own people were of early American descent. My grandfather was a civic leader, a Mason. Massena was a strong Masonic town. He was just ill over the thing. He said it was terrible that this happened. I think most people didn't believe any of this Jewish thing. They were just sick at heart about it." [17]

While all of this was taking place, Willie Shulkin turned up at the police station for questioning. The official report of Trooper McCann and Lieutenant Edward Heim of the Malone Company (along with a statement issued subsequently by Mayor Hawes) indicates that Willie "came to the police office" and "volunteered" information.[18] It seems unlikely, however, that the boy, in his mental state, would have done anything of the sort. If Eli Friedman is correct in his assumption that at least one of the highway patrolmen was snacking at Comnas's Crystal Palace, then Willie was probably taken in tow to City Hall. In any event, someone was dispatched to bring him in. We can only imagine the boy's excitement as he made his way down the slippery three steps to the side entrance of City Hall.

With Hawes and San Jule present, both of whom knew Willie and could have put a stop to the farce (later Hawes was to write, "It was evident he had a deranged mind"),[19] McCann put a series of questions to the boy. Willie's sisters, Dora Cohen and Mimi Klein, insist that "no local police would have bothered." [20] But McCann was new in town and probably did not know with whom he was dealing. Desperation, coupled with weariness, would have justified the interrogation. There simply were no other leads. As Heim's report states: "The troopers considered him of 'low mentality' and thought he might have been influenced by tales of a rumored custom in the olden days for members of the Jewish faith to offer a blood sacrifice." [21]

Did Willie know about the disappearance of the Griffiths girl?

Yes.

Did he have any ideas? Where she might be? How she had disappeared? Who was responsible?

Willie offered several "contradictory stories." [22] He went on in "a rambling manner" about possible kidnappers. Bootleggers. Gangsters. Even Indians. The Saint Regis Indians at Hogansburg.[23]

McCann tried to regain control of the questioning. The troopers "understood that this boy believed a blood sacrifice of Christian children was proper in connection with observance of the Day of Atonement." [24] Could Willie explain?

Such was the leading question put to a boy Dora Cohen describes as "impressionable" and "open to suggestion." Again, Willie attempted an answer, but became disoriented. McCann looked around. San Jule was shaking his head. Hawes clearly seemed embarrassed. The mayor motioned to McCann, and the two men walked to the front of the room, leaving Willie to regale San Jule, Hughes, and officer Demo with tales from Jewish history.

The State Highway Patrol report concludes: "After some conversation, officers realized the boy was of low mentality and sent him home with an officer." [25] What Willie had said was not totally dismissed, however. According to Mayor Hawes's account, "As a result of his statements, the local rabbi was asked to call at the police station." Hawes insists that he knew the rabbi would be "interviewed," but "I did not send for the Rabbi. I did not know the nature of the questions to be asked him and was not present at the interview." [26]

Someone must have urged the interrogation of Rabbi Brennglass, and it assuredly was not McCann. Things were moving too quickly for him. The idea that the Jews had plotted all this seemed fantastic. He would call on Brennglass only when all other possibilities were exhausted. In the morning. Meanwhile, he ordered Hughes to take Willie home and went out to resume the search of the Nightingale Section with the few volunteers he could muster. Mayor Hawes was not among them, however. He went home, convinced that a good day's work had been done. Later, Hawes would admit, "I was the one who got the discriminating idea first." [27]

7

Jake Shulkin tried to give Willie as much freedom as possible. So he wasn't surprised when he got
home from the store to find that his son was still out.
Willie's absences used to make his wife nervous, but
Jake would tell Sarah, "The boy's got to live his own
life. *Mann ken nisht tun alles far ihm.*" (You can't do
everything for him.) Privately, though, Jake himself was
rather concerned. Willie was a man now, but it wasn't
like talking to Ben. Ben you could discuss everything
with and he would understand. But Willie was like a
big, simple child. People would laugh at him or prod
him into trouble without his even understanding. Still, it
could have been worse. Willie could still be in that
place, that hospital.

When the doorbell rang, Jake was stunned to find his
son standing sheepishly beneath the porchlight next to a
police officer, a man Shulkin had never seen before.

The man quickly explained what had happened, apologized for the inconvenience, and left.

Willie's sisters, Dora and Mimi, have only vague recollections of that night. "We were rather sheltered," says Dora Cohen. "Something like that would be kept away." [1] They do recall how Willie's involvement caused a great *shishging* (commotion) in the household. Ben Shulkin concurs: "Willie didn't even realize what he had done. When he got home, he stayed in his room. But my father was aboil." [2]

This wasn't like that other time with Harold. That little girl was lost somewhere, and the police really suspected Willie. No, that wasn't exactly right. The police didn't know whom to suspect, but now the entire Jewish community was under question. Jake Shulkin went to the wall phone and dialed Sam Slavin's home number. The two men were more than business partners. Minnie Slavin had cared for the Shulkin children whenever Sarah fell ill (a more frequent occurrence as the children grew older), and the Slavins felt extremely protective toward Willie and Harold. Any problem that concerned either family could be handled in joint conference.

On any other night, Sam Slavin might have joked about Jake's call. Take a glass of schnapps, go to bed and forget about it. But not tonight. Minnie had just been talking with Jeannette Rosenbaum, and she had reported that toughs were going through the stores of the Jews downtown and that there was a good deal of excitement down at City Hall. The two men agreed that it would probably be best to get in touch with Joe Stone and see what ought to be done.

Like Shulkin and Slavin, Joseph Stone was a prominent figure in the Massena Jewish community. He was the principal stockholder in Stone & Co., which he ran with Eli Friedman and Saul Rosenbaum. A well-built man, taller (nearly six feet) than most Jews in town, he also enjoyed more education than most Jews or Gentiles in Massena. A graduate of McGill University in Montreal, he had a perfect command of English, and while Jake Shulkin may have served as president of Adath Israel congregation, it was Joe Stone who came to be recognized as the spokesman of the Jewish community. It was he who bailed out a traveling troupe of performers stranded in Massena. He was the "token Jew" secretary-treasurer of the village volunteer fire company. And it was Stone who most often could be seen at City Hall representing Jewish interests. The specter of a pogrom-ridden childhood in Galicia and the awareness that came with education that anti-Semitism could be combated with more than tears on this continent made Joe Stone, even more than Jake Shulkin, an activist on behalf of his people.[3]

An observant Jew, like most of his *landsmen* (co-religionists) in Massena, Stone was not in his store that Sabbath. The partners had arranged to stagger their weekend workdays. Like Sam Slavin, however, Stone had also been contacted by the Rosenbaums that evening and was slightly unnerved. He did not feel the matter should be dismissed. Nor did he feel that it compelled the calling of a meeting of the synagogue board. For one thing, the rabbi was in the midst of preparing for *Kol Nidre* services the next day. Besides, he reasoned that any late-evening convocation of Jewish elders might lend credence to the canard that they had been summoned for the very reason now being hinted at by bigots in town—the ritual vivisection of little Barbara Griffiths. Stone told Jake Shulkin he would be over shortly and suggested that Jake call Jesse Kauffman. The three of them would determine what to do.[4]

But for the presence of a tailor named Cohen who left town after an abbreviated stay, J. J. Kauffman was the only Jew in Massena in 1896. A recent immigrant from Bessarabia, he opened a dry-goods clothing store on Main Street right at the edge of the Grasse River. The shop still stands in near-toxic closeness to the water, expanded somewhat after forty years to embrace another building to its north. It is run by Kauffman's son, Abe, himself a graduate of Cornell, his daughter a graduate of Radcliffe. Intellect, tenacity, and charm, those were the chief traits that old Jesse transmitted to his offspring. A swarthy man given to overweight, balding, with twinkling dark eyes, Jesse had come to Massena when it was less than a boom town, in the days when Charles Warren had just begun to develop the locks on the Saint Lawrence River. When Adath Israel was founded in 1919, Jesse Kauffman became its first president.[5] It seemed only fitting that he should be privy to any decision affecting the fate of the Jewish community in town.

When Joe Stone arrived at the Shulkins' residence, Kauffman was already there, sipping tea. Stone had driven through town and was none too pleased by what he had seen. Massena seemed deserted but for a few hard-faced men clustered on several corners. That was unusual, even for 10:00 P.M. on a Saturday night. Stone recognized several of the men as "associates" from the volunteer fire department, the type that did not like him or his kind.

Once more, details of this crucial meeting are rather skimpy. Neither Minnie Slavin, Jack Jacobs, Eli Friedman, or novice historian Lou Greenblatt recalls the specifics. It seems probable that Stone, Shulkin, and Kauffman engaged in the traditional Jewish didactic of pilpul, the Talmudic casuistry, assessing a situation in a hairsplitting fashion.

There were, for example, two possibilities: either the girl would be found or she would not. If she were found, then again there were two possibilities: either she would be harmed or unharmed. If she were unharmed, everyone would laugh and go home, and nothing more would come of it. If she were not well, again two possibilities: either she would be dead or injured. In either case, who could say if a bear, a sadist, Indians, or Jews were responsible? And what if she were not found?

All three men had had personal experience with pogroms. The thought that "it" might happen in Massena, in the United States, was repugnant to them. Then Jesse Kauffman reminded his colleagues of what had happened in his brother Isaac's hometown, Kishinev, in April 1903. The Jews were accused of killing a Christian servant girl at Easter. There was never any proof that the Jews had had anything to do with it, yet the town's leading newspaper, the *Bessarabetz,* published the rumor. Police did nothing to suppress it. Leo Tolstoy and Maxim Gorky both denounced officials for their complicity in what happened. After two days, the *pogromchiks* left 45 persons dead, 86 wounded, hundreds of stores and homes gutted, dozens of women raped. They drove nails into the heads of women and babies, smashed their skulls against the walls of their shops. They ripped open the bellies of pregnant women, castrated men, cut the breasts off young girls, and hacked the dead to pieces like carrion in the streets. There were 50,000 Jews in Kishinev, one-third of the city's population.[6] Massena's Jews numbered only 100 in a community of 8,500.

When Jake Shulkin mentioned that all this had happened twenty-five years before in tsarist Russia, that pogroms could not occur in America, the scholar, Joe Stone, reminded him of the Leo Frank affair. The lynching of a Jew in 1915 might be dismissed because it had occurred in backward, bigoted Georgia,[7] but Stone recalled, moreover, that something like a pogrom had taken place in New York City in 1850. A Yiddish journal had detailed "the shocking incident":

> It was the eve of the Great Day of Atonement of the Jews and they were all in the synagogue. The house in which the synagogue is situated is occupied by both Jewish and Irish families. During the gathering of the congregation someone brought a streetwoman in to the rear of the building: a short time later, a rumor spread that the Jews had murdered a Gentile girl for their holiday. About 10:30, a crowd of some 500 men burst into the house, broke down the doors, and literally pulled from their beds sleeping women, one of whom was in childbed next to a sick husband. A most shocking riot was perpetrated; everyone who resisted was knocked down, a little box of jewelry to

the amount of 63 dollars was stolen from a peddler. The remarkable thing about this affair is that three Irish policemen were the leaders of this raging mob, and the tumult thereby acquired a sort of official character, whereas after all, the authorities had remained totally ignorant of this riot.[8]

There were almost 14,000 Jews living in New York City when the incident referred to above took place.[9] Reluctantly, Shulkin, Kauffman, and Stone concluded that the same kind of thing could happen in their town. Unsure how to proceed, they decided to contact the American Jewish Committee for assistance. Abe Kauffman says today, "My father called Louis Marshall of the American Jewish Committee. The reason was to send a report to the Committee and let it do what it will." [10] At the time, however, the men were not so self-composed. They were genuinely frightened that a pogrom was in the making and, according to Jake Shulkin, were "strong in our opinion that it is a national affair *k'lol yisroel.*" [11]

It was well past eleven when Louis Marshall got off the phone. Millionaire, philanthropist, crusading civil libertarian, he was the most reknowned of all Jewish leaders in the United States in 1928. The 40,000-member American Jewish Committee, which he chaired, was the most venerable of Jewish activist groups in the country, having been established on the heels of tsarist pogroms in 1906. Significantly enough, it was probably the richest, counting among its hierarchy bankers Jacob Schiff, Julius Rosenwald, Oscar Straus, and James and Paul Warburg, historian Cyrus Adler, and Judges

Mayer Sulzberger, Leon Sanders, and Joseph Proskauer, the latter one of Al Smith's closest cronies.[12]

The achievements of this organization were almost legendary among Jews. In 1911, on the heels of Russia's harassment of American Jews and the charge that a Jew in Kiev had committed ritual murder, Marshall and the others lobbied successfully in Washington for abrogation of a Russo-American commercial treaty that dated back to the age of Jackson. Three years later, the Committee took the lead, along with several Orthodox and labor groups in the United States, in establishing the autonomous Joint Distribution Committee, a relief organization whose purpose was to succor Jews in distress all over the world. From 1915 through 1967, the JDC spent nearly $1,000,000,000 on programs designed to assist stateless or persecuted Jews.[13]

Through all of this, the imprint of Louis Marshall was clear. In his thirty-five years as a partner in the firm of Guggenheimer, Untermeyer and Marshall, he waged a ceaseless struggle for human rights. That meant serving on slum commissions or as mediator in garment strikes in New York City, seeking payment of the bonus to veterans or higher workmen's compensation for the half-million Americans maimed in industry each year, advocating immigration reform and protection of the rights of Japanese, Hindus, and blacks in this country, and defending the right of members of the Socialist Party (he was a staunch Republican) to sit in statehouses or Congress. At the same time, Marshall never lost sight of his particular commitment to the Jewish people, a people he viewed only as a religious group. Like most assimilated Reform Jews in America, he had been weaned on the teachings of Rabbis David Einhorn, Gustav Gottheil, Kaufmann Kohler, and Isaac Mayer Wise, men who rejected the renaissant idea of Zionism. Though Marshall supported the right of Jews to settle in Palestine (or anywhere else, for that matter), he never endorsed the concept of a Jewish state in the Middle East.[14]

In 1919, Marshall headed up the Comité des Délégations Juives at Versailles. There he was placed in the incongruous position of having to press for guarantees for Jewish *national* minorities from the newly created states of Central and Eastern Europe. By 1928 the constitutional guarantees were already meaningless in Poland, Rumania, Hungary, and the Baltic states. But Marshall seemed to flit from one "triumph" to another. Just the year before the incident at Massena, the president of the American Jewish Committee achieved one of the great coups for Jewish rights in America. He elicited an unctuous apology from Henry Ford for articles published over the course of seven years in Ford's *Dearborn Independent*.

Of no small consequence, Ford's weekly had a circulation of 700,000 readers. Its editor, William Cameron, constantly fulminated against what he considered a Jewish-Communist conspiracy in America "which seeks to make the United States what it has already made of Russia." In a surrealistic reconstruction of history, plagiarized freely from the writings of Nazi economist Werner Sombart, the *Dearborn Independent* tried to show how Judaism contained a built-in profit motive and was responsible for the greedy capitalist system. Unsatiated by the birth of the new economics, Jews had gone on to exploit their unsuspecting neighbors by penetrating and controlling joint stock companies, mulcting the Gentiles who offered them protection and love. This was especially true in Colonial America, where Jewish storekeepers allegedly were unruly and unethical. It was so after the Revolution (the person of Haym Solomon was transmuted from a patriot who offered his entire fortune to help underwrite the war for liberty into a war profiteer), when immigration brought more Jews, more banking, more theft. Ford, who had an abiding hatred for bankers, anyway, permitted the text of these first polemics to be published in hardbound as *The International Jew.*[15]

The *Dearborn Independent* also lifted freely from *The Protocols of the Elders of Zion.* Supposedly a serious monograph published in 1905 by "Professor" Serge Nilus in Russia (alone enough to raise doubts as to its legitimacy), the manuscript had actually been authored during the middle of the nineteenth century by a Frenchman named Maurice Joly. Then titled "A Dialogue in Hell between Machiavelli and Montesquieu," it was intended as an attack against Napoleon III. Through Nilus's editing, however, what emerged was a free-wheeling assault against the Jews, who, it was alleged, were plotting to take over the world.[16]

According to Nilus, Paul Krushevan, Cameron, the *Dearborn Independent,* and Ford, the Jews recognized their weakness in numbers and physical strength. But secret instructions dictated by a conclave of their elders (the site of such a gathering is never disclosed) noted the inherent stupidity of the goyim (here used as a pejorative term for Gentiles). The goyim were "fools, babblers, would-be intellectuals, who had lost their power to reason and were nothing but a pack of sheep." Jews could gain ascendancy over them by craft. Gain control of monopolies and gold, and at the same time delude the workers by championing higher wages and better working conditions. Head up labor unions and lead strikes to drive out the little man and stifle the free-enterprise system. Ally with the Masons and defend freedom of conscience, relativism, Darwinism, Marxism, socialism, to undermine or erode the struts of the *goyisher* faith. Trumpet all kinds of glittering generalities, freedom, liberty, play on their sentiments. Gain control of the press because the media are necessary to propagandize the people. Worm into secret advisory posts at high levels of government. Champion inoculation and simultaneously spread disease among the goyim. Kill off their best racial stock in internecine struggles, while the Jews' allies and fellow Asiatics, the Japanese and Chinese, wait to overrun Western civilization. Foment revolution and internal dissention just as Jews had done in causing the collapse of Periclean Athens (!), the Roman Empire, imperial Spain, and the Bourbon monarchy in France. Lest someone suspect the master Jewish scheme, ransom the major cities of the world through another device—subways, Jewish-planned and secretly mined.

Then, at the appointed hour, the Kingdom of Zion will be declared. In a single day, the enemies of the Jews will be exterminated, including "those goyim who know too much" and the international dictatorship headed by a Davidic king-pope will be declared. In that kingdom there will be no rights for anyone except the right to be dehumanized. In this slave state, Jewish lords will enjoy absolute control over the press, education, economy, and politics. The only religion permitted will be that of Moses. Universities will be emasculated, study of the classics prohibited. Society, taxed beyond its wildest imagination, with property taxes, income taxes, capitation taxes, will be permanently shackled by the Jewish gold standard. To keep people in line, society will be under the close scrutiny of secret police. But to ensure quiet among the people, their rulers will keep them pacified with bread and circuses, the dole, welfare, guaranteed incomes, along with spectacles, arena affairs, sporting matches, and mass circulation of pornography.[17]

Among the Jews in America who felt personal outrage at the printing of such slanders was Aaron Sapira, the leader of a large agricultural movement in the Midwest. Sapira charged defamation when the *Dearborn Independent* accused him by name of being a participant in "a conspiracy of Jewish bankers who seek to control the food markets of the world." With the support of Marshall and the American Jewish Committee, Sapira instituted a million-dollar suit for damages against Ford and his journal in March 1927. Shortly afterward, another Jew, Herman Bernstein, claiming defamation in connection with articles published about the *Protocols,* brought a $200,000 libel suit against Ford and his publication.[18]

Early in June 1927, Louis Marshall was approached by Ford's spokesmen, Earl David and Joseph Palma, who indicated their chief was willing to issue a public apology to the principals and Jewish people if the

American Jewish Committee withdrew its suits. Marshall must have felt vindicated, for on June 30, 1927, Ford offered his apology. "To my great regret," he declared, "I have learned that Jews generally and particularly those of this country, not only resent these publications as promoting anti-Semitism, but regard me as their enemy." Maintaining that he was unable to give attention to all facets of his vast empire, Ford admitted he had given much attention of late to the problem of anti-Semitism and had concluded that much of what had been published stemmed from gross forgeries. "Had I appreciated even the general nature, to say nothing of the details, of these utterances, I would have forbidden their circulation without a moment's hesitation, because I am fully aware of the virtues of the Jewish people as a whole, of what they and their ancestors have done for civilization and for mankind toward the development of commerce and industry, of their sobriety and diligence, their benevolence and their unselfish interest in the public welfare." Ford emphasized that his retraction was made with sincerity and was voluntary.[19]

In accepting this apology, Louis Marshall published a letter of his own to Ford, a letter that recounted the travails of twenty centuries of insults, injuries, persecution, and intolerance. "Happily such excrescences could not flourish on American soil," Marshall wrote. Neither the press nor the public at large treated the charges made in the *Dearborn Independent* seriously. But for Jews who suffered a horrible past, the canards evoked nightmares and tortured memories. Marshall was pleased that a gentleman like Ford had awakened to the dangers of such tales, and in the Jewish spirit of forgiveness hoped for his future friendship and goodwill. "It is my sincere hope that never again shall such a recrudescence of ancient superstition manifest itself upon our horizon," Marshall concluded.[20]

Though some Jews may have regarded Marshall as a herald of the messiah, the Ford affair reeks. The historian Norman Cohn points out that Ford's apology was drafted for him by Marshall, that Ford suddenly took out $160,000 worth of advertisements in Yiddish newspapers (heretofore of no interest to the Ford Motor Company) as a form of "hush" money, and that Ford's solicitous attitude was prompted not so much from a genuine change of heart as from concern for the success of the new Model A. The Ford Motor Company was in the process of retooling and could not afford to have capital tied up in court cases that it would eventually lose.[21]

At the same time, it smacked of presumption for Marshall to speak not only for American Jewry but for Jews all over the world. His satisfaction level was not necessarily equivalent to that of a Jew in Düsseldorf or Stettin who within seven years would face the reality of a Nazi leader who regarded *The International Jew* as one of the greatest books ever written.[22] Adolf Hitler was never dissuaded by Ford's retraction, nor was the anti-Jewish hayseed from Oklahoma or his citified cousin in Yorkville, New York City. Long after the momentary impression of an eloquent apology had faded, the memories of seven years of gutter insults remained with the common folk.

In the topsy-turvy world of the 1920s, nothing should have surprised Louis Marshall. He knew, for example, that most Americans resented Jews as neighbors, workmates, schoolmates, or in-laws, that many believed Jews smelled bad, that they were greedy, pushy, clannish, loudmouthed, cowardly, slothful, and lecherous.[23] Not just in Grant Wood's America, but along New York's Park Avenue one could hear tales of Jews with tails or goat's feet. The historian Joshua Trachtenberg reported meeting one Kansan who refused to believe he was Jewish because Trachtenberg had no horns projecting from his head.[24] There were legends in Utah, New York, Kentucky of the Wandering Jew—Lazarus, Ahashuerus, Malchus, by whatever name he was known—the pathetic figure who had flogged Christ before his crucifixion and was doomed to roam the face of the earth to the end of time.[25] And occasionally there were reports of violence—vandalism, beatings, burnings. The Leo Frank affair in 1915 even had ritualistic overtones. It was the purpose of the American Jewish Committee to see that things never got to the stage they reached during the Frank affair, "to prevent the infraction of the civil and religious rights of Jews in any part of the world," and "to render all lawful assistance and take appropriate remedial action in the event of threatened or actual invasion or restriction of such rights." [26] In the seventeen years that Marshall headed up the organization, it seemed to be doing just that, against seemingly insurmountable odds.

American Jewish Committee records had nothing on a blood-libel accusation in this country before Massena.

THE INCIDENT AT MASSENA

People may have muttered the thought aloud at cocktail parties or taverns, and Georgia Senator Tom Watson had hinted at the possibility during the Frank affair, but Louis Marshall could not recall a time when law-enforcement officers had paid any mind. It never got beyond the "Christ-killer," "Jewboy," "well-poisoner" name-calling stage. What made the news from Massena all the more disturbing was the fact that authorities there were actually encouraging belief in the lie. And with Yom Kippur coming on. Marshall agreed with Kauffman and the others that this was a smear directed not only against the Jews of Massena but against all Jews, against God on His most sacred of days. It could not be ignored.

And yet Marshall must have wondered whether this all could be exaggeration. After all, he hailed from Syracuse and liked to believe he knew how people upstate, Jew and Gentile alike, thought. Poorly educated merchants from Europe might see things larger than life, might tend to distort facts. Their concern seemed real enough when he spoke with them on the phone. But they couldn't expect a man of Marshall's stature to race northward on their near-hysterical evocation. This late. On *yom tov*. The insult had to be investigated. It would be impossible to get someone from the American Jewish Committee executive offices this late on a Saturday, or, for that matter, over the holidays. Since the Massenans had called him, he would not bother to notify the heads of the other principal activist organizations—the Anti-Defamation League of B'nai B'rith, the American Jewish Congress, or the Jewish Labor Com-

100

mittee. Nor would anyone be available at the offices of
Der Tog, The Forward, The Morning Journal, or
Freiheit, the Yiddish papers.

The best organization to check out the matter was the
Jewish Telegraphic Agency. This was the wire service
established for Jewish newspapers, synagogues, and organizations in The Hague in 1917. After World War I,
the JTA had transferred its headquarters to London,
then to New York.[27] Its best man was Boris Smolar. A
serious young reporter from the Ukraine, Smolar had
witnessed the agonies of a Jewish community threatened by ritual murder during the Beiliss affair of 1911–
1913. Smolar had been in this country only a few years,
so his English was somewhat murky, but he wrote well
enough in English and Yiddish, and what he wrote was
done with a passion that gripped his readers. His sense
of *Judenschmerz* (Jewish pathos or empathy) enabled
him to commune with fellow ghetto-dwellers on New
York's Lower East Side.[28]

Smolar was in bed when his phone rang that night.
As he recalls it, his conversation with Louis Marshall
went like this: "This is Louis Marshall ... something
very important and urgent. ... I just received a long-
distance telephone call from Jewish leaders in Massena,
a small town in the upper part of New York State. ...
The tiny Jewish community there is in panic. ... A
Christian four-year-old girl disappeared, and the Christian population is excited. ... Ugly rumors are being
spread that the Jews kidnapped the child for ritual
purposes for Yom Kippur. ... A ritual-blood libel

against the Jewish community is in the making. . . . The Jews are in mortal fear. . . . Can you take the first train and proceed immediately to Massena?" [29]

Smolar was flattered that Marshall had thought of him. "The matter was of extreme urgency," he recalls, "the first blood-libel accusation against American Jews in the history of the United States." [30] Prompt action was commanded, and Marshall wanted a report as quickly as possible. Smolar rushed to dress, then grabbed the first train north to Albany out of Grand Central Station. In his haste, he packed sufficient clothes for only one or two days.

The trip was an incredibly slow, tedious, frustrating one. In Albany, Smolar switched trains and boarded a night "milk train" that plodded the remaining 200 miles through the Adirondacks. There were long delays at junction towns like Colton, Hannawa Falls, South Hammond, and Norwood. Another change. Hunger. The smell of grease and leather and smoke. The swaying of a primitive coach that left one without sleep, but with a touch of *mal de mer*. And through it all, the curiosity, the dread of what was actually going on in Massena. Smolar did not arrive in Massena until noon the following day.[31]

8

*I*t had been only twelve hours since Barbara Griffiths disappeared into the Nightingale Section, but when dawn broke through the cinnamon-tinged clouds over Massena on Sunday, many people had even forgotten her name. She now was "the girl" or "the victim" or "that poor little kid." Her father lay collapsed on a living-room sofa while a few men continued to slog through the swamp paddies looking for her. Cole Cummins recalls, "There was a little lull. The search had died down. The men got sick of tramping around. It was a mystery that they hadn't found her. They thought they'd covered all the territory." [1]

The handful of citizens who attended church that chilly morning were treated to the most perfunctory of religious ceremonies. Though nearly everyone in town had heard that the Jews were "implicated," not one of Massena's Gentile clergymen from Saint John's Episcopal, Sacred Heart, First Methodist, Emmanuel Congregational, First Baptist, or Advent Christian churches offered to explore and explode the ritual-murder canard this Sunday. According to Cole Cummins, "There were regular church services, but I don't recall the ministers particularly featuring this incident." [2] Saul Rosenbaum adds, "As a rule, the ministers said, 'Boys, sing a few songs, go home, and have a good time.' " [3]

Massena was waking up. The previous night's searches of Jewish shops had not sated the curiosity of the vigilantes. They returned to the downtown sector to rub dust from the windows of Kauffman's, Levine's, or Shulkin and Slavin's to gaze into cellars that were better illuminated in the daylight. Men, women, and children with grim faces, their arms crossed or their hands in their pockets, filtered back to City Hall to wait. Their number had grown to three hundred by 10 A.M.[4] Every now and then, Fred Holiday, Massena's sixty-year-old stringer for the *Syracuse Post-Standard,* would wander through the crowd into the police station, inquiring if anything more was known. Not to be outdone, L. C. Sutton, the ultraconservative publisher of the *Massena Observer,* kept his handsome (if a bit too toothy) cub reporter Leonard Prince (just one week in town) on call at City Hall. They were all waiting for news that had to come.

The same atmosphere of imminence and tension permeated the Jewish community. Boris Smolar states that upon his arrival "The Jewish stores were closed, and no Jew was seen on the street, obviously aware of the dangerous atmosphere." [5] It was, of course, Sunday, and no Jewish stores would have been open, anyway.

Moreoever, Massena's Jews tried to act nonchalant, normal, as if nothing were out of the ordinary on this *Erev* Yom Kippur. Joe Stone picked up the Montreal and Syracuse papers at a downtown drugstore, just as he had done every Sunday for two decades. Teenaged Jack Jacobs went out of his home on Orvis Street to visit a friend. J. J. Kauffman's son, Abe, played a round of golf at the country club, just as the Klansmen were poring over his father's store a second time.[6]

Despite efforts to make things appear normal, there was an awkwardness to these actions—as if the Jews knew they were being observed and were mechanically, consciously performing when they left their homes. Like medieval Jews at Easter, some stayed home, locked their doors, and waited. Fear and anxiety were the dominant emotions in the homes of people who had come from Bessarabia, Galicia, or Volyhnia. As Jake Shulkin wrote later, "Each of the members of the small community was in a state of dispair [sic]. Each could imagine only the worst results because the excitement in the city was intense and each knew from history what the blood accusation had cost us." [7] This was not just some game. They knew that when people starting whispering ritual murder in the Old Country, the next step in such semantic exercises was to expect screams of "Kill the Jews!" And twenty or thirty years of peaceful coexistence in this town in America did not count for much. Convince yourself that any hoodlum or vandal that invaded your home would be punished by the law, and that still would not make the situation any more palatable. What good would his subsequent punishment do a maimed child, a dead wife? It was now that mattered, and Massena was so isolated it might just as well be a shtetl in the Pale of Russia. Certainly its police and mayor were no better than the *Haidamaky,* Ukrainian Cossack irregulars. They were even engineering this farce.

All through that Saturday night and Sunday morning, the telephone was their link. It sustained them, scattered as they were on so many streets about town. The phone, at least, diminished the feeling of being alone and helpless. Saul Rosenbaum might have fantasized that his two-story stucco home might be a veritable fortress, a Masada if need be, but that did not help his wife, Jennie. A pretty young woman with neatly bobbed brown hair and blue eyes, she could not understand how any of this had happened. Saul had lived through it in Europe. But she had been born and raised in New York City. This was America. It was impossible that people could say such things about Jews and that Jews should fear for their safety. The Jewish women of Massena identified with Marion Griffiths in more ways than one that night. What if the little girl were found injured or dead? Jennie Rosenbaum asked herself. The Rosenbaums had a baby girl of their own, one year old. What would *they* do to her? Mrs. Rosenbaum did not sleep that night.[8]

Over at the Slavins', Minnie Slavin was on the phone much of the morning, trying to calm her neighbor around the corner. She was worried, too, but Sam Slavin exuded confidence. While small in size, he warned that anyone who tried to do anything to him or his family would have to go over or through him.[9] At the Shulkins', Willie was in his room, oblivious to what was going on. Jake Shulkin was on the phone—talking to Jesse Kauffman, to Joe Stone (who had given up any pretense of interest in world news), to Rosenbaum, old Mr. Jacobs, Slavin. Sarah Shulkin was sick to her stomach.

Morris Goldberg knew nothing of the town's excitement as he made his way to Alcoa that Sunday morning. Fortyish, balding, with a slight physique, Morris was one of the few Jewish workers at the plant. Starting as a common laborer, he had been put in charge of the transportation garage. He worked in close company with many of the townsfolk, including at least one of the men who had been at Comnas's restaurant the previous evening. The man may have recalled Goldberg's speaking about Jewish rituals at work.[10] In any event, it was at the urging of this unnamed "citizen assistant" that Trooper Hughes was sent to Goldberg's home about ten-thirty in the morning to question him about the possible kidnapping of Barbara Griffiths.[11]

The two men were informed by Mrs. Goldberg that her husband could be found at Alcoa. There, in the plant garage, Trooper Hughes put a series of questions to him. According to Jake Shulkin's report of the incident, "The trooper asked him if it is true that the Jewish people in the old country use human blood at the holiday services, passing it to the members of the congregation." [12]

Of all the Jews in Massena, Morris Goldberg was in the unique position of being able to squelch the libel before it grew any worse. Here was a man who was well-liked and respected by his Gentile neighbors. Like most Massenans who lived in the constant tension of this "tolerant" community, Morris Goldberg made an effort to show people Jews were no different from them. They, too, worked hard, kept their homes clean, loved their children, treated their wives with deference and tenderness, were quiet folk. At the same time, Goldberg liked to puff up his image before his *landsmen* through his unflagging attendance at Adath Israel. Ritualistically faithful, scrupulously observant—that was the impression Morris Goldberg tried to convey. If anyone might dispel the rumor, it would be he.

In actuality, a worse champion of Judaism was hardly imaginable. Born in the slums of New York City, Goldberg was reared in a Gentile orphanage. There he was made aware of his Jewish background, but was given only the skimpiest appreciation of history or ritual. By the time he arrived in Massena, he was abysmally uninformed about both aspects of Jewish life. His fellow congregants treated him as little better than a *shabbes goy,* a Gentile with a Judeophile streak, he knew no Hebrew or Yiddish, struggled to follow the instructions during a service. Among the Jews of Massena, he was regarded as a status-seeking illiterate.[13]

Again, Trooper Hughes put the question to Goldberg: Had he ever heard of Jews using human blood in their rites? Goldberg's response: "I don't know if such a custom exists in the old country, but in this country they don't have this custom." [14] Pressed for further information, Goldberg told the trooper he did not know much about it. If more information was desired, he suggested contacting Jesse Kauffman or the rabbi.

Shortly past noon, Mickey McCann put through a call to Rabbi Berel Brennglass. Speaking as cordially as possible, the trooper asked the rabbi to come down to police headquarters. "He desired to have a conversation and obtain important information." [15] Brennglass, who, amazingly, had not yet been informed by anyone of the charge then pending against Massena's Jews, replied that he would be right over.

Why McCann decided at this point to summon the rabbi is not difficult to appreciate. McCann had been up all night, operating under great pressures, without any success. As he noted subsequently, "I was terribly excited and fatigued at the time, having been on duty for many hours without food or rest." [16] Highly susceptible by now to even the most extreme suggestion, McCann decided to pursue the investigation along the lines advocated by Mayor Hawes. The mayor supposedly was still in bed at the time and would disclaim responsibility for what was to transpire.

Rabbi Brenglass left his old frame dwelling at 180 East Orvis Street and made his way to City Hall, a distance of no more than 300 yards. Brennglass was another of those pugnacious little men who had gravitated to Massena after the great Atlantic crossings at the end of the nineteenth century. Born in Troky, Lithuania, in 1876, no more than five feet two inches in height, a slim 125 pounds, with the traditional salt-and-pepper beard that marked the East European *rebbe,*

Berel Brennglass had actually made the trip across the ocean twice. He was nearly forty years old when he returned to America in October 1915 with his wife, Eva, and four children to take up permanent residence in New York City.

Somewhere along the way, though, he had contracted a touch of tuberculosis. In 1918, on the advice of his brother, who was then a well-known New York physician, Brennglass removed the family upstate "to a better climate." One of the major convalescent spots at the time was Saranac Lake, and Brennglass's first congregation was at Tupper Lake, no more than 50 miles from Massena. When Adath Israel was founded in 1919, it lured Berel Brennglass away from his mountain retreat.

For more than two decades, until his wife died of cancer in 1941, Brennglass was the dominant force in the religious life of Jews in Massena. A one-man Sanhedrin, he would not tolerate any slackening, any digression from strict Halakic tradition. During his tenure, there was not one intermarriage between Jew and non-Jew in town. Most Massenan Jews kept kosher homes and observed the Sabbath, walked to synagogue, and were found at prayer and not in shops on holidays. Brennglass had grown up in a town that was a center of Karaism (biblical fundamentalism) and was as distrustful of that fanaticism as he was concerned about the menace of assimilation. In either case, he believed such ideas meant the decay of Judaism. And for this reason he emphasized the traditional, rabbinical approach to Jewish life. It is a testament to his labors that Massena was, and still is, regarded as the most religious, most Orthodox Jewish community north of Syracuse and

Utica. As rabbi, Brennglass was more than a philoso-
pher of religion. He was a true *moreh* (guide, paceset-
ter), like the Hasid whose flock emulated his every
action because they believed him to reflect the actual
standards of heaven.

Brennglass was not, however, a man who lived *in
vacuo*. A well-read gentleman, he would accompany his
youngest son, Samuel, to the village library each night
to read the latest issues of the *New York Herald-Tribune*
and the *Times*. (Samuel recalls that frequently they
would have to wait until Cole Cummins, the resident
intellectual of Massena's Gentil community, had finished the papers.) The rabbi was quite fond of his children and took special pride in Samuel, who was the first
Jew to serve as manager of the Massena football and
basketball teams and to be class valedictorian of the
high school (in 1927). The last accomplishment was all
the more remarkable since Samuel, who was away at
the City College of New York when the Griffiths child
disappeared, was only fourteen years and ten months
old when he graduated from high school. He graduated
from college with honors at the age of eighteen and
subsequently went on to serve as law secretary with
Irving Lehman before establishing himself as one of the
more prominent attorneys in New York City.

Because he demanded so much of everyone he knew,
some people did grumble about the rabbi, whose hair
smelled of Ivory soap and whose speech was thick with
the gutturals of Eastern Europe. The younger children
in town were especially hard on him. Because they were
forced to perform in cheder in much the same way as
children in the Old Country were, their memories of

Brennglass, his harsh methods, and the inconvenience of attending services when there were more inviting diversions—picnics, ball games, snowball fights—are not quite so benign. Some even maintain that Berel Brennglass was not a true rabbi, that he was never ordained, that he was nothing more than the town shohet (ritual butcher). One person told me, "Look, in a small town what you need is someone who can kosher meat. After that, who cares if a person has graduated from a seminary?" [17]

Actually, Brennglass was a graduate of one of the better religious academies in Lithuania, the Slobodka Yeshiva outside Kovno. But it was in his capacity as shohet that he left the greatest impression on some of his students. His dual role of rabbi-butcher may also have contributed to the negative image that some of Massena's Gentiles had of Jews in general.

Done properly, *shehitah* (ritual slaughtering) is probably more humane than the process of flaying animals that have previously been stunned and are twitching in agony. The process (outlined in Genesis 4:4, Leviticus 1:5, 3:10, and Deuteronomy 12:21) owes its origins to the Jews' repugnance for blood or eating anything contaminated by blood. Even today, traditional Jews prefer their meat cooked to the point where it resembles shoe leather more than beef. Blood is regarded as the source of life, the *nefesh* (spirit). To drink such a substance would be only one step removed from cannibalism. To tame the Jew, to implant in him the horror of bloodshed, ancient teachers took the process of killing animals from the individual and gave it to the professional shohet. Because of this, writes A. Leroy Beaulieu, "Consider the one circumstance that no Jewish mother ever killed a chicken with her own hand and you will understand why homicide is rarer among Jews than among any other human group." [18]

The purpose of *shehitah,* then, is total blood catharsis. Three things are required: an eligible performer, the proper instrument, and a killing stroke correctly administered to the animal. The operative must be a pious Jew, never a Gentile, thoroughly versed in the ritual, someone who has secured a *kabbalah* (written license) from a rabbi. Non-Jews, deaf-mutes, idiots, drunks, women, or old men whose hands might tremble cannot qualify. The shohet, generally a butcher, must also review his rites every thirty days.

The shohet must possess a *hallaf,* a knife free of the slightest notch on the blade, one whose keenness is tested by passing it between the fleshy tip of a finger and a nail. These implements, menacingly large, rectangular objects of the purest steel, are contained in simple wooden boxes. They also must undergo periodic examination by a rabbi. They are enough to frighten someone who does not know their purpose.

The third part of *shehitah* requires a skilled cutting stroke, through the jugular, windpipe, and gullet, virtually to the backbone of the animal. It must be applied quickly and with certainty to the cartilaginous area of the animal's throat, between the trachea and lungs, the region that disgorges the greatest amount of blood and thereby purifies the animal. Any hesitation, extra pressure from fingers, burrowing, slipping, tearing, or deviation from the specified zone renders the animal *nebelah* (unclean, as if it died of natural causes). Once it is properly slaughtered, the animal's lungs are inspected to determine if it had some loathesome disease. All blood is then buried by a layer of dirt or ashes, and a blessing is chanted.[19]

Ritual slaughtering has always aroused visceral reactions on the part of those who do not understand it. Ancient Romans who did not wince at gladiatorial combat, medieval Christians who partook of the body and blood of Christ, antivivisectionist Nazis—all attempted to suppress it. Even today, many sophisticated Westerners, hearing of the process for the first time, consider it barbaric and inhuman and have tried to pass laws requiring the preliminary stunning of animals. They do not understand that such stunning causes brain and membrane damage before death, diffuses blood throughout the body, and makes the animal *treyfeh* (unclean). A government as enlightened as Switzerland's passed anti-*shehitah* legislation in the 1890s and, as mentioned earlier, the legislature of Connecticut considered a measure to outlaw this "bestial" practice in 1928.

People cannot comprehend that *shehitah* may actually be more merciful to the animal because it is quicker and cleaner than the accepted Western slaughterhouse style of killing. This may very well be the crucial point. For Gentiles, the slaughter that went on in the pens of Chicago or the fens of Kent was always remote, removed from town and from sight. Until Upton Sinclair shook them back into reality, Americans blocked out the consumption germs on the floor of the slaughterhouses, or the dead rats in the sausages, or the artificially rejuvenated hams or porks. Gentile slaughterhouses were always out of the way, and people did not see animals convulsively twitching on hooks. But kosher butchers were easily seen, on New York's East 105th and Delacey streets, in Pittsburgh's Squirrel Hill, or, in Massena, on Orvis Street in the person of Berel Brennglass.

All the Jews of Massena kept their own chickens, but when they wanted them slaughtered they brought them over to Rabbi Brennglass. People saw him go out to the old piano box he had in his backyard and return with the dead birds. Occasionally he would slaughter a cow. And even though they were farm people, these people in Saint Lawrence County, the entire thing had an eerie quality to it, a barbarism they could not accept. It was simple to fantasize that the rabbi might just as easily take a little child out back and slash its throat with impunity.

If his neighbors had seen him the previous day, they would have shuddered as Rabbi Brennglass went through the rite of *shlug kapporus.* An archaic ceremony performed by the Orthodox the day before Yom Kippur *shlug kapporus* is the act of taking a live chicken, its feet bound, and waving it thus over the head of adults and children, all the time saying, "This is my *kapporus,* my atonement, for the sins of the previous year." It is done in the home before the fast of Yom Kippur. Then the bird is killed and made into soup for the feast at sundown at the end of the Day of Atonement. Symbolic of ancient sacrifice, the animal is shared with the poor, who are given the gullet, wings, and neck. The ceremony is still practiced by certain Orthodox sects and Hasidim, while other Jews prefer to ease their consciences by donating cash to charity at this time of year.[20]

Very likely, the rabbi was not even thinking of *shehitah* or *shlug kapporus* as he approached City Hall. If Lee Friedman's account is anywhere near accurate, Brennglass must have been terrified by what he saw. According to Friedman, "At the police station a mob swirled aimlessly. . . . Massena's handful of police was at a loss how to handle the crowds. . . . Their meager jail accommodations precluded the possibility of arresting the entire Jewish population, yet something had to be done, and done promptly and boldly, to calm the general tumult." [21] Other sources agree that a mob of 300 to 400 persons "in a state of unusual excitement" were milling about the police station.[22] When the little man in the rumpled brown suit strode forward, a cry went up: "Oh, there's the rabbi! At last!" [23]

Brennglass walked quickly through the mob and entered the police station by the same side door Willie Shulkin had taken. He was greeted by Chief San Jule, who motioned one of his subordinates to show the rabbi into a smaller room that served as San Jule's office. Brennglass was told that a trooper would come in shortly. Left alone, the rabbi stood looking out the window, contemplating the strange crowd assembled on Main Street. Just then, a state trooper entered the room with San Jule. The chief introduced Mickey McCann and walked out, leaving the door open.[24]

The two men exchanged pleasantries, and McCann even offered the rabbi a cigarette (which the older man politely declined).[25] McCann then went on to review the events of the previous twenty-four hours surrounding the disappearance of Barbara Griffiths. He further explained that Mayor Hawes had suggested calling in the rabbi.[26] Naturally, the rabbi offered all assistance in the recovery of the little girl. McCann expressed appreciation for the offer, but that was not quite why he had called in Brennglass.

McCann: "Is tomorrow a big holiday, a fast day?"

Brennglass: "Yes."

McCann: "Can you give any information as to whether your people in the Old Country offer human sacrifices?"

Brennglass (indignant): "I am surprised that an officer in the United States, which is the most enlightened country in the world, should dare to ask such a foolish and ridiculous question."

McCann: "Was there ever a time when the Jewish people used human blood?"

Again the rabbi answered in the negative, explaining that not only human blood but animal blood, too, is forbidden.[27] According to Lee Friedman, "To the impatient officials he [the rabbi] could cite chapter and verse of Holy Scripture, from Leviticus and Deuteronomy, to prove that not only was it enjoined by holy law 'thou shalt not kill,' but that a conforming Jew would submit to the worst of torments rather than allow human blood to touch his lips." [28] Noah and his descendants had been forbidden to consume the blood of animal flesh (Genesis 9:4). So too, Aaron and the priests of Israel were commanded "throughout your generations, in all your dwellings, neither to eat fat nor blood," (Leviticus 3:17) for "the blood is the life" (*hadom hoo hanofesh;* Deuteronomy 12:23). God had commanded, "I will set my face against that soul that eateth blood and will cut him off from among his people, for the life of the flesh is in the blood" (Leviticus 13:10). And there were other citations on blood and the koshering of meat that any literate person could find in the Old Testament: Leviticus 3:17, 7:26–27, 11:2–8, 19:26; and Deuteronomy 12:23–25, 14:4–6. Brennglass was shaking with emotion when he finished his tirade.

McCann tried to muster a smile. "Please don't think the idea originated with me," he stammered. "Somebody else, a foreigner, impressed me with it."

Brennglass demanded to know the source of the charge. "This is a *rekhiles,* a slander against the entire Jewish people," he exclaimed as he was escorted to the door. McCann said he was sorry, that the rabbi could go, that it was all a mistake. But Brennglass went on, "I am not through with you yet! You will have to reveal the name of the party who gave the information, that he should be taught he is not in Poland or Rumania!" [29]

He had been in the station for only a few moments, but Brennglass's ordeal was not yet over. As he climbed the steps to Main Street, his path was blocked by those who had tried to witness the inquisition. People who recall the scene liken Brennglass to a little David menaced by several Goliaths. "Three-fourths of the rabbis we've had since that time would have collapsed under the pressure, "Jack Jacobs told me. "But not Berel Brennglass. He was an extraordinary man, tremendous, a man of amazing courage." [30] Lou Greenblatt compares the rabbi with Lenin. "He was short, slight, about the same build of Lenin, with the same goatee but more hair. He used the same sort of fiery gymnastics, oratory as Lenin. There was even spittle coming out of his mouth when he spoke." [31]

"What do you people want?" the rabbi shouted at the crowd. "What are you doing here? Isn't it bad enough that a little girl has been lost? Why aren't you looking for her instead of standing around? You should be absolutely ashamed of yourselves. By what nerve do you insinuate such things against your Jewish neighbors? Would you call in a Catholic priest and question him? Go home before somebody gets hurt. Go home and pray to God that He'll forgive you for what you are thinking!" [32]

The speech was brief, the words were simple, and yet they had at least a temporary mollifying effect upon the crowd. Says Cole Cummins, "The rabbi really laid those fire station fellows out." [33] People drew back to make way for the little man with the agonized face and tear-stained cheeks as he made his way home to prepare for *mincha* (afternoon prayers) and *Kol Nidre* that evening.

9

It was a hellish afternoon for Rabbi Brennglass. Any thoughts of working on a traditional Yom Kippur sermon were dispelled in the atmosphere of terror that had settled over Massena. How to speak of forgiveness or absolution when the very survival of the Jewish community was at stake? Instead of *Kol Nidre,* chanting the *Borechet Hagomal* (the blessing upon deliverance from peril) would be more appropriate tonight.

Following a brief *mincha* service (the second of the statutory daily prayers for Jews, lasting no more than twenty minutes), Brennglass and other Jewish leaders—Rosenbaum, Stone, Kauffman, Shulkin, Friedman, and Slavin—convened at the rabbi's home. They had come to discuss strategy, and once more the traditional Jewish hassling ensued. Despite the threat to them all, the meeting was disrupted by semantic disagreements, non sequiturs, long discourses into irrelevancies, and the exception, always the exception. Why didn't Jake Shulkin keep his boy at home? Why should he? Why should the police listen to a *meshumed* like Goldberg? What do you expect? Haven't we treated him like a Turk? That's all besides the point! Should the people stay home tonight and not go to synagogue? [1]

From the viewpoint of safety the idea of bypassing *Erev* Yom Kippur, the most sacred of Jewish nights, had great merit. But Rabbi Brennglass would not have it. *Pogromchiks* or hooligans notwithstanding, Jews must not cower or hide. Services would begin shortly before sunset, just as they had since the inception of the Mosaic code, and everyone, including women and children, must attend. Someone suggested that a committee visit the mayor and police chief to ensure the safety of the congregants, but Joe Stone hastened to point out that the rabbi had already tried to enlighten McCann, without apparent success. Little help could be expected from official quarters. What of the call to the American Jewish Committee? They had been promised action, but nothing had happened. New York must have dismissed the affair as crank hysteria.

Finally, it was determined that additional distress calls should go out: a wire to Rabbi Stephen Wise of the American Jewish Congress; a detailed letter to Marshall (perhaps the written word would not be ignored); a phone call to Julius Frank, a prominent Jewish businessman and onetime mayor of nearby Ogdensburg; and another call to Lieutenant E. F. Heim, McCann's immediate superior at the Malone battery, requesting that he come to Massena that same day. Invariably these requests concluded: "We do not know how to proceed. We request that you immediately inform us what action to take." [2] Today, Eli Friedman says, "We made a mistake contacting both Marshall and Wise." [3] Back in 1928, Massena's Jews could not anticipate the "diplomatic" fiasco that would ensue from seeking assistance from the two giant egos of American Jewry.

By 3:00 P.M. the men had finished drafting their plans. Life would go on with as little departure from the norm as possible. As the group broke up, Eva Brennglass came into the parlor and announced the arrival of Boris Smolar of the Jewish Telegraph Agency. It was one of the few things that had happened to buoy their spirits. At least somebody in New York was taking note of the serious situation.

Smolar recounts "As I was sitting with the rabbi in his home later, listening to what happened during the police interrogation, and telling him that I came all the way from New York at the request of Louis Marshall, a group of Jews suddenly burst into his house shouting jubilantly: 'The child has been found! The child is alive!" [4]

Across town, Dave Griffiths had continued the search. His anger at having slept through half the morning had subsided. Now there was only a numbness, a feeling of unreality, as if the past twenty-four hours were merely a bad dream. The quiet, even flow of this life had been irreparably jarred, and now, trudging through the woods with George Ure, it was almost as if none of this had happened. It was easier to fantasize that this was merely another hike, a hunting expedition, an overnight camping trip. Intentionally, he focused his mind on little things—trees, stones, mudholes—but it was impossible to shut out the sound of that pretty voice and the image of his daughter's twinkling eyes. He wouldn't let himself think of what might have happened to her. Griffiths had heard the rumors afloat in town, but he didn't pay much attention to them. Understandably, all he wanted was his child, alive and well. Each passing hour made that possibility less likely.

Sometime after three in the afternoon, Griffiths was called back to the residence on Cherry Street. He had been told by another neighbor who found him tramping dejectedly through the Nightingale Section that Trooper McCann wanted to see him. Griffiths still defends Mc-Cann's peculiar actions that weekend, maintaining that the officer was quite kind and that he received unfair criticism for merely doing his duty. "He hadn't been out in the bush," says Griffiths, "but he probably was running down leads in his car. He probably looked twenty-four hours, too, but he also had his other work to do. I don't even know where San Jule was. I didn't see the police chief." [5]

McCann wanted Griffiths to come down to the police station "to help with clues." McCann savored that word, *clue* as if somewhere in "any past information" there was a key word or action that would suddenly unlock the engima.

As they drove downtown, McCann asked, "You heard about the Shulkin boy?"

"Yes."

"Had him and the rabbi in for questioning. Nothing to it, though."

"I didn't think so," was all Griffiths said.

McCann shook his head. "Yeah, well, I'm in trouble now. The whole Jewish community is up in arms." [6]

Griffiths really could not have cared less about the mistakes McCann had made or what the haters in town were whispering. He only wanted his child back.

Sixteen-year-old Julia Phillips and fourteen-year-old Maud Hutchins had come in that morning from Norfolk to help in the search. The girls spent several hours in the fields, doubling back and forth, romping with other teenagers, playing games of tag, picking wild berries. Many seemed to regard the search as an excuse for a frolic. Now the girls were sitting by the roadway on Andrews Avenue, Route 37, near the Casaw farm, less than a mile from town. It was nearly 4:00 P.M., and time to go home.[7] They hoped to hitch a ride with someone who might carry them the ten miles south to Norfolk.

Just then, a small figure emerged from the dense brush and trees in a clearing no more than fifty yards from the three maple trees where the girls were resting. It was the only possible place where an individual might be visible from the roadway.[8] The girls looked at one another, unbelieving, then leaped to their feet, shouting, "Barbara! Barbara!"

The little girl with burrs in her hair responded with a smile.[9]

Shortly afterward, Julia Phillips flagged down a car dirven by W. E. Timmerman, and the group drove back into town. The news that the Griffiths girl had been recovered passed through town like an electric wave, and cheers and laughter replaced the sullen glares of the afternoon. Says Dave Griffiths, "We were down at City Hall talking when the news came. We were all delighted. McCann brought me from the police station to my home. There was a big crowd around the house." [10]

Barbara regaled her relieved audience with how she had gone looking for her brother, Bobby, and failed to find him. She kept looking, and when it grew dark and cold, she crawled into some tall grass to keep her legs warm. And then she fell asleep. During the night, she woke up several times, but it was still dark and she was afraid to move. It rained, but she was unaware of this until she awakened with the sun shining and found her dress wet. She determined to go home, but did not know the way. So she kept on walking, stopping occasionally to rest, until she met the "nice" girls. Asked whether she had seen any of the hundreds of people who had been looking for her for the past twenty-four hours, Barbara innocently replied, "No, but I saw ever so many cows." [11] Another version has her saying, "No, I didn't see any people. I did see a big bear and two little ones, but I didn't move." [12] And still a third source, Eleanor Dumas, declares, "She heard the men, all right, but she didn't hear her mother's voice, so she didn't answer." [13]

Whatever the case, the girl was home. Her clothing had some tears from where she had snagged it on branches and burrs. She was tired and hungry, and a little frightened (according to Mrs. Griffiths, Barbara slept with the light on for several weeks afterward). But according to Dr. MacAloon, Barbara was "none the worse for the experience." [14]

THE INCIDENT AT MASSENA

It was an extremely happy and grateful Dave Griffiths who released the following statement to the press:

> Mrs. Griffiths and I desire to avail ourselves of this first opportunity of publicly expressing our deep gratitude and sincere appreciation of the wonderful response of our townsfolk in aiding us in our trouble. We are aware of the hundreds of men who spent hours, both day and night, searching for our lost child. We cannot thank all of you personally. This is impossible. But we want you to know that your efforts are appreciated by us. Such evidence of genuine friendship can only make us more fully appreciate the spirit of friendship and neighborliness in this community. In times of sorrow or need, the people of Massena always respond to the occasion. They have done this for us.[15]

The incident should have been closed.

Massena City Hall. (This photo depicts refurbishment by the WPA in the 1930s.) The mob gathered here, outside the basement headquarters of the village police. Inside, the authorities questioned Rabbi Brennglass about whether the Jews offered human sacrifices. *(Courtesy of the Massena Town Historical Society)*

Police Chief Floyd San Jule. He offered his facilities to State Troopers McCann and Hughes as a command post. *(Courtesy of the Massena Observer)*

Mayor W. Gilbert Hawes. He would later admit, "I was the one who got the discriminating idea first." *(Courtesy of the Massena Observer)*

Eli Friedman, standing before the entrance to Adath Israel Synagogue the following spring. *(Courtesy of Mimi Shulkin Klein)*

A later photo of the synagogue. The sidewalks had been blocked by toughs.
(Courtesy of the Massena Town Historical Society)

Louis Marshall of the American
Jewish Committee wrote to
Mayor Hawes, ". . . this apology
must be couched in such terms
will meet with my approval. . . .'
*(Courtesy of the American Jewish
Committee)*

Rabbi Stephen S. Wise of
the American Jewish
Congress. He would cross
swords with Louis Marshall
more than once. *(Courtesy
of the American Jewish
Congress)*

10

Back in 1928, there were few buildings on Church Street. Some homes. The Hotel Nadeau down at the Andrews Avenue end of the road. And Adath Israel up at the other end. There had been only a few changes in the stark two-story red-brick building that had housed the Congregationalist faithful for almost a century. One still entered the house of worship from a crumbling brick platform, now reinforced by a black tubular railing. But the steeple that proclaimed the building a church had been removed in 1919. Above the simple twin outer doors of oak there was now a *Mogen Dovid* (Star of David) and capital letters that proclaimed ADATH ISRAEL SYNAGOGUE. Light filtered into the sanctuary from large square windows, at least four feet high, on the southern and eastern walls. The building contained no more than fifteen rows of pews (their filials in coxcomb style), sufficient to seat the entire

THE INCIDENT AT MASSENA

Jewish community of Massena but no more impressive than a deteriorating neighborhood shul (synagogue). Oddly enough, for a synagogue that prided itself on its orthodoxy, Adath Israel's ark, a lovely red-velvet-draped shrine, was located on the western wall, contradicting the rule that such shrines should be placed on the eastern wall, in the direction of Jerusalem. Necessity, availability of the building, dictated such an adjustment to the "Spanish" mode of synagogue.

The sun was setting as Massena's Jews, in accordance with the ancient instruction that worship commence when they could delineate three stars in the twilight heavens, made their way to the synagogue. As they walked across the Grasse River Bridge, past Massena High School, or down Andrews Avenue Hill, their mood was one of exhilaration. It was a gorgeous fall night, clear and brisk. With all the fears of the morning, the calls and letters that had gone out in anger, they could not help but feel as if today were their Purim. As Boris Smolar put it, "The joy of the Jews in town was indescribable. Their Yom Kippur prayers that evening and the following day had a special meaning for them. They saw a miracle in the fact that the child was found just a few hours before the Kol Nidre services." [1]

Such elation was premature. As each family arrived, they were disheartened by the presence of more than a hundred idlers in the vicinity of the synagogue. Gentile townsfolk, including the ubiquitous Roy and Willard Countryman and their fire station followers, were strung out the distance of a city block from the rear of the police station to the decrepit Hotel Nadeau. As the Jews passed by, these toughs deliberately blocked sidewalks and shouted a sarcastic "Hello, Saul!" or "Hi, Jake!" to people they never would address by their first names, as if announcing arrivals to a Hollywood premiere.

It was as if nothing had happened since Rabbi Brennglass had tried to disperse the ugly mob that noon. If anything, the earlier silence had been transmitted into open bluster. It was now that volunteer firemen suggested running the Jews out of town. Now that insidious cracks against "kikes" and "sheenies" and other obscenities were uttered. Now that the shadowy figures challenged their Jewish neighbors, "Scared you into returning the girl, didn't we?" [2] As Jake Shulkin later noted, "Now the rumor is broadcast that after questioning the Rabbi the guilty [sic] became frightened and gave up the child." [3] Such were the comments that greeted the Jews of Massena as they entered their synagogue that night to atone for their sins, to atone for the sins of their fellow Jews, to atone for the sins of all mankind.

Jewish tradition has it that when all else in this world is destroyed, when there is no Temple, no altar for atonement, no other festivals of any kind, Yom Kippurim, the Day of Atonements (plural) will still remain, a permanent day of reckoning for all mankind. "And it shall be a statute for ever unto you in the seventh month on the tenth day of the month," reads the Book of Leviticus of this most sacred day in the middle of the most solemn period of Jewish worship.[4]

It is significant that the Yom Kippur service begins with the chanting of *Kol Nidre,* a haunting melody whose antiquity is demonstrated by its Aramaic opening words: *"Kol Nidre, veesore, vacharome, v'konome, v'chinuye, v'kinuse, ushvu'os."* "All vows, bonds, devotions, promises, obligations, penalties, and oaths: wherewith we have vowed, sworn, devoted, and bound ourselves; from this Day of Atonement unto the next Day of Atonement, may it come unto us for good; lo, all these, we repent us in them. They shall be absolved, released, annulled, made void, and of no effect: they shall not be binding, nor shall they have any power." The Jew seeks forgiveness for all vows falsely sworn through the past year and for those that might yet be undertaken in the year now beginning. *"Nidrono lo nidre."* (Our vows [to God] shall not be vows.) *"Veesorono lo esre."* (Our bonds shall not be bonds.) *"Ushvuosono lo shvuous."* (And our oaths shall not be oaths.) [5]

No mean exercise in perfidy, this. It is a chant etched in the blood of thousands of Jewish martyrs who sought an end to persecution at the hands of Muslims or Christians in the Middle Ages by openly converting to those faiths while secretly practicing the worship of their fathers. It was the song that sustained the Marranos—the "swine," as they were called by Spanish Christians, the *Anusim* (forced ones), as their fellow Jews referred to them, the *conversos* (converted ones), as they preferred to call themselves—as they tried to survive the purge of Jews from the Iberian Peninsula. More than 200,000 would be hunted down, massacred, exiled from the land they had inhabited for 700 years before the coming of the Visigoth "Spaniards." More than 200,000 would be accused of feigning Christianity, and from their number another 20,000 would be burned in the *sambenitos* (sackcloth) of heretics at well-attended public executions. In the secret meeting places where Jews congregated each year, whether in Toledo, Granada, Kayrawan, or Cairo, they would chant *Kol Nidre* to affirm their faith in the one living God, to make their agonies more bearable. God would see through their daily charade, would understand that they were blessing the Virgin or performing the *salat* (formal Muslim prayer) in order to stay alive. And He would forgive them on the Day of Atonement for such vows falsely sworn, forcibly taken.[6]

In seeking absolution from God, however, Jews must atone not merely for their sins of commission but also for all actions that they have *omitted* in the past year. The hardened heart, the loose lip, lack of chastity, deceit, despising of parents and teachers, presumption, violence, profanity, foolish speech, lying, bribery, scoffing, gluttony, usury, arrogance, obstinacy, contentiousness, lust, lechery, envy, false levity, bearing tales, swearing vain oaths, hatred, cowardliness, idolatry—all of these are sins that are enumerated not once but several times on Yom Kippur and that are recited for the purpose of impressing the penitent with his record.

A unique confession, this Jewish confession, for it is an annual affair of incomparable solemnity. The Jew who has tried to make his communion with God throughout the year must now make amends for all that he has forgotten or concealed. More than that, he must bear responsibility for his fellow Jews who have not behaved in a manner consistent with the Mosaic Code. If a Jewish slumlord goes out and collects rent for a vermin-ridden apartment from a tenant whose children fall prey to the bites of rats, *all* Jews are responsible for this sin, for having failed to influence the landlord. Collective responsibility applies to all Jews. Even more, collective responsibility extends to the sins of all mankind, Jew and Gentile alike. "And all the congregation of the children of Israel shall be forgiven, and the stranger that sojourneth among them; for in respect of all the people it was done in error." [7] Like the mythical *lamedvovnik,* the Jews congregate and pray for forgiveness of all men's sins. Not presumption but a desire to restore justice and harmony in God's universe underlies the Jew's actions.

How difficult it must have been for the Jews of Massena to have spoken the words "Thou dost graciously give knowledge unto man and teachest mortals understanding" or to invoke His blessings upon "thy people Israel at all times and in every hour with thy peace." With what had happened in the past twenty-four hours, however, most of them must have prayed with special feeling the traditional: *Ovenu malkenu, batale machshevos sonano."* (Our Father, our King, annul the designs of those who hate us.)

Kol Nidre. The congregation rose for the *Borechu,* blessing God's name, and the *Shema,* the basic Jewish credo testifying to His unity. *Veohavto.* "Thou shalt love the Lord thy God with all thy heart, with all thy soul, and with all thy might." The instruction for Jews to teach their children the commandments, to nail *mezzuzot* to their doorposts, to wear "fringes" on their garments as reminders of God's covenant. *Michomocho.* Recalling the wonders performed for Moses and the Children of Israel and their hymn of thanksgiving.

Reader's *Kaddish,* sanctifying the name of God. Then the long *Amidah* (silent prayer) of repentance. *Mogen Avot* (Our Father's Shield). The opening of the ark and more responsive readings. The *piyyut* of Rabbi Yom Tob of York, martyred in 1185. A recitation of sins in alphabetic form. *Yaaleh.* "O, may our sorrows rise to Thee at nightfall. Our anguish reach Thy presence from the dawn." God of our fathers, God of Abraham, Isaac, and Jacob, Refuge of our mothers, Helper of the tribes, Father of orphans, Judge of widows, "Answer us, O Lord, answer us." [8]

When his congregants had again sat down, Rabbi Brennglass spoke from the *bimah* (the raised platform or stage that contains the desk for reading the scroll of law). Behind the *bimah* stood the ark with ten Hebrew letters, symbolic of the commandments, etched in wood. In traditional medieval synagogues, the *bimah* was located in the middle of the building. Because Adath Israel had been a church, Massena's Jews had adapted the old altar and apse to their needs. Old-timers recall how the *bimah* jutted out six to eight feet into the pews, as if someone felt it necessary literally to bring the word of God to the people.[9] Flamboyant orator that he was, Brennglass hardly needed this.

Few people can recall the exact words the rabbi used that night, but it is not difficult to reconstruct the principal themes of his speech. Jake Shulkin recalled he would not be quieted even after the girl was found, and the encounter with the hoodlum element surrounding the synagogue did nothing to calm his state.[10] Even the young people who did not understand all the rabbi's

Yiddish were transfixed.[11] Says Ben Shulkin, "He laid it on heavy. He talked about ritual murder. That it can happen here, even with good government." [12]

No great scholar, Brennglass began by reminding people how the Day of Atonement was instituted, how in the Book of Leviticus (16:25) it was commanded: "Ye shall afflict your souls and shall do no manner of work, the home born or the stranger that sojourneth among you." True, in connection with these rites, the Lord had commanded sacrifice (a sprinking of the blood of a bullock or a goat, Leviticus 16:14–16; a burnt offering of unblemished bullocks and rams, Numbers 29:7–11). Only the most superstitious of people would believe that a primitive animal sacrifice practiced 3,000 years ago, before the Jews even possessed Jerusalem or a Temple, could represent a commandment demanding human sacrifice. Only the most ignorant of people would believe Jews imbided human blood after all the biblical proscriptions against this. But despite biblical laws and papal disclaimers, Gentiles still believed Jews capable of such heinous acts, at every season—Purim, Passover, and now Yom Kippur. It had happened before, in Europe—in Spain, Poland, Rumania, and Russia. And now, sadly, it had even happened here.

Brennglass was confident that God would not abandon His people in this "day of affliction." Exact parallels for Massena's ordeal could be found in Torah portions for this week. Referring to the section *Vay Elech* (Deuteronomy 31:6) recited the previous day, the rabbi exhorted his listeners "Be strong and of good courage. Fear not, nor be affrighted at them, for the Lord thy God, He it is that doth go with thee. He will not fail thee, nor forsake thee." So, too, the "stumbling block" referred to in tomorrow's reading (Isaiah 57:14) would be cast out of the way. *Haftorah Haazinu,* to be chanted the next Sabbath, also painted a picture of gloom—the people Israel confronted by waves and snares of death, assailed by the floods of Belial, surrounded by the cords of Sheol (abode of the dead). But the people called out to God, and "He delivered me, because He delighted in me. The Lord rewarded me according to my righteousness. According to the cleanness of my hands hath He recompensed me."

The medieval poet had said, "Endure this; muzzle yourself and be silent; for if you answer a fool, you will hear more things." Brennglass advised his people to engage in no debates or shouting matches when they left the sanctuary. "Just as God will forgive us, so must we, too, forgive our neighbors. We must forgive because it would be false pride if we did not. For transgressions committed by man against man, man forgives. But 'Elohim,' the Divine Judge, will judge him.

"We must forgive, but we must never forget. We must forever remind ourselves that this happened in America, not tsarist Russia, among people we have come to regard as our friends. We must show our neighbors that their hatred originates in fear, and this fear has its roots in ignorance—ignorance of Judaism, our beliefs, our history, our people, our God. We must show them they have nothing to fear from us. We must tell the world this story so it will never happen again." 13

The rabbi now called upon the people to recite the traditional prayer for our country, invoking blessings on "all who exercise governmental authority" to do so "in

justice and equity." It is a prayer to make America a
land of influence for good throughout the world, fulfill-
ing the visions of the prophets. Among the verses of this
Tefillah baad Hamemshalah was one of special significance that night for the public servants and citizens
of Massena: "Unite all inhabitants of our country,
whatever their origin and creed, into a bond of true
brotherhood to banish hatred and bigotry and to safe-
guard the ideals and free institutions which are our
country's glory."

11

"*V*im *ruchi, g'viyosi, adonai li, v'lo, iro,*"
(And though my body I forsake, I rest in the Lord in
fearless calm.)

It was well past ten when the strains of *Adon Olam*
(Lord of the World) had subsided and the emotionally
drained people could leave Adath Israel. The cool night
breeze and the length of the service, it seemed, had
discouraged all but a handful of stragglers, who continued to wait and watch outside, as if their vigil might
bring down a thunderbolt or two upon the building.

It may have helped that one of those who stood at the
steps of the synagogue was Lieutenant Edward F. Heim
of the State Highway Patrol. Mickey McCann's superior
from Malone had forgone a comfortable Sunday with
his family after receiving a call from Joe Stone, and had
driven the 35 miles to Massena. A tall, handsome man,

with more than the normal intelligence of officers assigned to the North Country, Heim was eager to close the incident. The timely appearance of this uniformed officer was sufficient to dispel any notion entertained by some toughs of disrupting the Jewish service.[1]

As people filed out of Adath Israel, Heim inquired where he might find Stone. He was eager, he said, to clear this thing up right now. The only thing he really did not understand was how the charge ever originated. Stone, Eli Friedman, and Saul Rosenbaum offered to give the trooper an education while they walked about town. Rabbi Brennglass, exhausted by his ordeal and facing a twelve-hour session in synagogue the next day, was excused.[2]

As the four men walked, somehow the streets they had known for more than a decade seemed unfamiliar, hostile. Orvis, Danforth, Bridges, Main, Laurel, Glenn. Earlier in the day, it would have been impossible for three Jews to attempt such a stroll. Now they had their special protective amulet, a state trooper, and he was bing treated to a short course in Jewish history.

Joe Stone explained what the ritual-murder charge was, how historically it had been the source of humiliation and brutalization of Jews in hundreds of different communities. When Heim asked how it could have originated, Stone suggested it may have come from the biblical injunction against the use of blood. In the minds of simple folk, the Jews seemed to "protest too much." Such emphatic prohibitions could be interpreted to mean that the Jews were really trying to conceal their true lust for gore, just as Tacitus had claimed the Jews' prohibition against eating pork was a guise for the secret worship of pigs.[3]

It may have been, Stone continued, that the charge originated with the circumcision or *shehitah* rituals, both of which continue to repel Gentiles. During the Middle Ages some Jews served as intermediaries in the slave trade between Europe and North Africa and kidnapped and castrated Christian children. Some were impressed into service for European monarchs as executioners. During the same period, as today, the foremost physicians in the world were Jews. They were the ones who more than any others dealt with life and death in an age of primitive medicine, in an age when bleeding a sick patient was a recommended practice. The bitterness of those who lost loved ones in such an epoch is reflected in the belief prevalent among the medical faculty of the University of Vienna as late as 1610 that Jews were required by their religious law to kill one of every ten Gentile patients.[4]

There was even an element of projection in all this, Stone pointed out. Christianity has always been sensitive about the doctrine of transubstantiation. There was that difficult passage in the Gospel of John: "Except ye eat the flesh of the son of man and drink his blood ye have no life in you." Early Christians had rushed into pagan arenas to smear themselves with the blood of martyrs. Such blood, it was believed, possessed a divine numen (spiritual force). Throughout the ante-Nicene period, the Christian Mass had been lampooned by enemies as an unholy, cannibalistic rite. Tertullian, Origen, and other early Church Fathers complained of the ignorance and superstition of pagan masses who could not understand the mysteries of Christianity. Throughout the Middle Ages, Christian peasants gorged themselves on blood pudding. How natural for a religion once slandered to transfer that slander to another religion when its own success has been assured.[5]

There was no question that some Christians had continued to believe in the efficacy of blood. In 1507, for example, a group of Dominicans and Franciscans had denounced one another for using the blood and eyebrows of a Jewish child for magical reasons. In 1890, in Galicia, a Polish "magician" had been accused of snatching two Jewish cadavers to extract blood necessary for the exorcism of a peculiarly "Jewish" type of typhoid from a peasant's hut. Stories of a similar vein were too numerous to relate.[6]

Heim listened with fascination as the three men explained the factors that nurtured the ritual-murder libel. The love-hate psychopathy within the Christian Church toward a sister faith. The deicide charge against Jews who allegedly tortured the Christian messiah, a charge revived every Easter with the prayer for the "perfidious Jews." Mundane considerations figured prominently, as well. The Jews loaned money to monarchs at low interest. Raising the charge of ritual murder relieved the lord of his debts. At the same time, the "victims" would be canonized and the Church would reap a profit at their shrines. And, finally, there was ignorance, always ignorance. Somewhat inaccurately, they told Heim that in Europe when cases like this occurred, the police at least helped the Jews. It was the masses that stimulated pogroms against them in the Old Country. In fact, often as not, as in the case of the Kishinev pogrom, or those in Balta in 1881, or Odessa in 1905, or Proskurov in 1919, or Damascus in 1840, it was the officials themselves who planned and implemented the massacres.[7]

The point they were trying to make to Heim was that in some instances there were kindly police who warned the Jews in advance, and even a rare priest or muzhik (peasant) who tried to intervene on their behalf against the *pogromchiks.* Never in America had elected officials or the police sanctioned such a crazy idea, never until this day.

"Heim could see very clearly that there was no truth to the charge," Eli Friedman told me. "He readily grasped the significance of the officials helping and promised to work on the matter and resolve it as quickly as possible."

Lieutenant Heim wanted to summon a meeting of the synagogue elders, the rabbi, Mayor Hawes, Corporal McCann, and Chief San Jule for Monday morning.

"Tuesday," said Joe Stone.

Heim was surprised. "Why Tuesday? Why not tomorrow? I thought you wanted to clear this all up immediately?"

Because," Stone said softly, "tomorrow is Yom Kippur." [8]

At 2:00 P.M., Tuesday the twenty-fifth, Lieutenant Heim led a group of somewhat hesitant, contrite figures into Adath Israel for a special meeting with the town's leading Jews.[9] It probably was the first time any of the Gentiles had entered a synagogue in their lives. Corporal McCann, quiet, withdrawn, his career on the line, was still smarting from the words of his superior ("Why did you muck it up? I sent you here to keep the law, not to cause a revolution. What the hell's the matter with you?"). Chief San Jule, still embarrassed, still thankful he had not been charged with responsibility for the mess, was looking forward to two weeks in Vermont with his family, two weeks that would take him far away from Massena. There was Mayor Hawes, uneasy, his legs suddenly made of rubber, speaking excitedly, gesturing with his hands as he sought advice from the fifth member of the group, Town Supervisor Andrew Hanmer.

The latter, a fairly tall man with narrow, deep-set eyes, a gaunt, lined face, heavy jowls, and jagged yellow teeth, had, according to his son Seward, "the only brains in town." [10] Basically self-educated (he spent a year at Albany Law School before going out to clerk), Hanmer hailed from Little Island in the Adirondacks. In about 1907, he heard of the opportunities in the North Country, took horse, wagon, and children, and opened his own law practice in Massena. Fearless, conscientious, stable, thrifty (the family owned a modest home on Elm Street), he converted his book-lined office on the lower landing of the Central Building into the mecca of Republican politics. The Republican Party dominated Massena in those days, and Hanmer, fourteen years a town supervisor (comparable to a township trustee and/or county commissioner), dominated the Republican Party.

If Lieutenant Heim was miffed with McCann, Hanmer was even more put out with Hawes, whom he regarded as little more than a semieducated boob. The mayor's actions threatened to stigmatize the community as a refuge for superstitious yahoos. Worse, it could lead to trouble in the upcoming Presidential election. There were 2,000,000 Jews in New York State, and something like this was all that was needed to swing all their eligible voters into the Smith column. That very day, Tuesday, Hanmer had been visited by Julius Frank, the Democratic mayor of Ogdensburg, who had warned him the incident was viewed as "politically motivated" and "could have serious repercussions." [11]

Hanmer sat in the synagogue and listened with pursed lips and disgust as Hawes kept repeating, "You have to understand. I made a horrible blunder. It really wasn't the way it sounds. They've distorted the whole thing. I really didn't think it would come to this." [12] Hanmer had not participated in the hunt for Barbara Griffiths, had discounted rumors of a Jewish plot when he heard them, and resented having to do penance for something hatched by someone like Hawes.

Awaiting the delegation of officials were Rabbi Brennglass, Joe Stone, Eli Friedman, Jake Shulkin, J. J. Kauffman, and Saul Rosenbaum. It was not a happy group. The previous day's meditations had helped create a *cordon sanitaire* in time from the unhappy events of Sunday. The intense meditation and concentration on piety during Yom Kippur had helped soothe their feelings. But now they were dealing with reality again.

For more than two hours, the events of the weekend were rehashed in an emotionally charged atmosphere. Heim acted as the principal conciliator, trying to mollify Jewish representatives by pointing to the urgency of finding Barbara Griffiths and the necessity of chasing down all possible leads. His apology was deemed too shallow, insincere, and its very tone after his previous expressions of sympathy and understanding served to provoke Brennglass, Stone, and Shulkin. All of them were of a mind that the Ku Klux Klan lay behind the affair.

Heim's change of heart was apparently prompted by a belief that since peace had been restored to the community, any further dispute would merely stir up more hostility. He was not naive, and yet the lieutenant did report to his own superiors: "We tried to explain to the committee the reason for asking the question, but the committee seemed to take the attitude that this question was agitated by some organization to bring criticism on the Jewish church and its members in Massena and several told of its world-wide significance." In fact, Joe Stone had stated that the matter had already been reported to an attorney in New York City, and that they would be guided not by the advice of Lieutenant Heim or Supervisor Hanmer but by that other unnamed attorney. "We offered them apologies," Heim noted, "and feel the matter is closed." [13]

It was hardly that simple. The session also proved to be a heated inquisition of Mayor Hawes, the man Jewish leaders blamed for the rumor's gaining official sanction. The many versions of what Hawes said disagree in details but concur in that at Hanmer's urging he offered an apology, which the Jews rejected. Abe Kauffman recalls his father had Hawes saying with some degree of self-control, "Look, I acted like a damned fool. We're all friends. We're all in business here together. I'm sorry it happened." [14] A more extreme picture of the mayor's contrition was painted in a letter from Joe Stone to the American Jewish Congress later that week. According to Stone, the mayor "exhibited great mental agony and there were tears in his eyes" when he said, "I feel I have done wrong. I am very sorry that such thoughts ever entered my mind. I am ready to resign from my position." [15] Far different still is the image conjured up by Hawes's own statement to Jewish leaders published in the first week of October 1928. Here, the mayor stated, "I told them I regretted the incident occurred and if I had done anything in the matter which was insulting to them or reflected on their religion that I offer an opoligy [sic] and again repeat that as my position." [16] Hawes went on to say that he felt he was being accused of something he was not responsible for. "I have daily business intercourse with Jews and am on friendly terms with them. I have never entertained feelings of prejudice against them, and there is no hostile feeling against them in Massena." The mayor concluded "So far as I know, the incident is not generally known in Massena and any publicity must come from the Jewish people." [17]

Such publicity would not be long in coming.

12

"*M*um's the word." [1] That, supposedly, was the prevailing attitude in town during the next week, an attitude reflected by Mayor Hawes when he later wrote: "It is not a matter that is being discussed in Massena and very few people know anything about it and if it gains publicity it will only be through the Jewish people of Massena." [2]

Despite the efforts of police and other officials to suppress knowledge about the incident, the situation in town did not revert to normal. Chamber of Commerce Secretary Ernest Wagar recalls that many people reacted "with disgust" [3] when they learned of the libel. There were numerous quarrels among adults, spats between Jewish and Gentile schoolchildren.[4] "Everyone took sides," says Seward Hanmer, "and local people boycotted Jewish merchants." [5] Friends of Hawes resented the Jews' obstinacy in refusing to accept the mayor's generous apology, for telling him "the matter is out of our hands." [6] Sales in Jewish stores skidded as the boycott lasted more than two weeks. And there are those willing to testify that Hawes himself vindictively led the boycott. According to Saul Rosenbaum, "The mayor stood outside the door of our store and told people not to go in." [7]

Back in New York, Boris Smolar informed Louis Marshall that the case had a "fortunate ending." Smolar notes that Marshall was pleased, but adds that the head of the American Jewish Committee was "greatly upset" over the fact that the rabbi had been summoned to the police station.[8] Marshall demonstrated no great haste in doing something about his "upset." Not until Monday, October 1, eight days after Brennglass had been interrogated, was he spurred to action. Just the previous day, the *New York Post* had carried a story quoting Marshall on the Presidential race and bigotry. As if empowered by some heavenly force, Marshall had "cleared" both Hoover and Al Smith of charges of prejudice and decried the menace of intolerance in this country.[9] On this day, however, his attention returned to the Massena incident.

Marshall's three-page, single-spaced, typewritten letter to Major John Warner, superintendent of the State Police at Albany, was typically eloquent and presumptuous. Marshall recapitulated the circumstances of Barbara Griffith's disappearance, the rumor-mongering and excitement in Massena, the interrogation of Rabbi Brennglass, and the pogrom mentality of the mob even after the girl's return. For all this, he especially blamed Mayor Hawes and Trooper McCann, and openly questioned whether the latter ("so guilty of recklessness and lack of ordinary common sense") should remain on the State Police force. It was fortunate, wrote Marshall, that the girl was found "before official irresponsibility culminated in mob violence." [10]

Marshall went on at length to educate Major Warner in the history of the ritual-murder charge. "It was shown that of all people on earth the Jews were from the very beginning forbidden to eat even animal blood," he declared, citing the passages in Genesis, Leviticus, and Deuteronomy where this prohibition stands. He pointed out that the most distinguished popes in history and some of the foremost non-Jewish historians (such as Professor Thomas Masaryk of the University of Prague) had characterized the ritual-murder charge as "a brutal and inhuman falsehood." Even when the tsarist government marshaled all its energies against "a simple Jew" (Mendel Beiliss) in 1913, Marshall emphasized, "the greatest authorities in the world testified that there was not even the shadow of a reason to support such a belief." [11]

Marshall sought to do more than enlighten Major Warner, a graduate of Harvard, a Catholic, and just coincidentally Governor Al Smith's son-in-law. Like the frightened Jewish citizens of Massena, he, too, regarded the incident as a national affair. He made this point very clear the next day, October 2, in a public release to the New York press. Just as he had threatened Henry Ford with a substantial defamation suit the previous year, so now Marshall charged Hawes and McCann with "one of the most shocking exhibitions of bigotry

that has ever occurred in this country." He threatened
to sue these men for their "vile slander," "wanton attack
on Jewish honor," and "unspeakable calumny" unless
they first apologized (and were sincere and did not
mouth unctuous or vacuous phrases) and then resigned
from their positions as public servants.[12]

In his scathing letter to Hawes, Marshall stormed:
"What has occurred does not merely affect the Jews of
Massena, whose very lives were placed in jeopardy, but
the entire Jewish population of this country and of the
whole world is directly concerned in putting down the
abominable superstition which, due to your action,
might have resulted in one of those many calamities
recorded on the bloody pages of Medieval and even
modern European history. The very thought that public
officials in this day and age can seriously entertain the
idea that adherents of one of the great religions of the
world practice human sacrifice is an abomination and
betokens unfitness for public office." [13]

In demanding public, written apologies from Hawes
and McCann, Marshall warned further: "This apology
must be couched in such terms *as will meet with my
approval* [italics mine], so that the world may know that
the remorse which you have expressed is genuine. As
further evidence you should also resign from the office
which you now hold. Unless you shall at once pursue
one or the other of these two courses, I shall regard it to
be my duty to institute proceedings which I have been
authorized to take under Section 36 of the Public Officers' Law before the Appellate Division of the Supreme Court for your removal from office on the

ground of official misconduct. I shall wait for a few days for an indication from you as to whether it shall be necessary for me to adopt the latter course." [14]

Why had Marshall written the letters? He had known for some days what had happened in Massena. Boris Smolar's report merely confirmed the letters of Shulkin, Brennglass, and Stone. What really caused him to speak out, however, was the knowledge that Rabbi Stephen Wise and the American Jewish Congress were already actively engaged in the affair. Marshall could ill afford to be upstaged by Wise and his organization.

It was not the first time the charismatic rabbi from Oregon had crossed swords with Louis Marshall. Wise had been imported to New York City in 1906 to head up the prestigious Reform Congregation Emanu-El. Shortly thereafter, he broke with the board of trustees in one of those perpetual fights over who really should lead the congregation. The President of Emanu-El's board, who prompted Wise to establish his own Free Synagogue on New York's East Side, was Louis Marshall.[15] Again, in August 1915, hearing of massive persecutions of Jews by Russian and German troops along the Eastern Front, Rabbi Wise demanded action by the American Jewish Committee and the Joint Distribution Committee. At the time, the AJC soft-pedaled the reports of pogrom, and Wise walked out and formed his own American Jewish Congress. More heavily oriented toward a Zionist solution to the world's "Jewish problem," the Congress had as its declared purpose: "defining methods whereby in cooperation with the Jews of the world, full rights may be secured for the Jews of all lands and all laws discriminating against them may be abrogated." [16] Though financially weaker than the American Jewish Committee, the Congress's numbers would grow until it could report 700,000 persons had cast their ballots in a World Jewish Congress election of June 1938. The man who headed the American Jewish Committee when Wise took the masses out and left the impression that the American Jewish Committee was a rich man's organization was Louis Marshall.

Stephen Wise was an activist. A longtime friend of Franklin Roosevelt, he would press for special immigration visas for German Jews at a time when Marshall's cronies, the Warburgs, were telling the President that Hitler was a passing phenomenon. It would be Wise who would organize the first worldwide boycott of German goods in 1933 in retaliation for Nazi brutality toward Jews. Wise, again, who would guide American Jewry peacefully, if ineffectually, through the guilt-ridden epoch of the Holocaust as president of the Congress, chairman of the American Emergency Committee for Zionist Affairs, chairman of the Executive Committee of the World Jewish Congress, cochairman of the Zionist Organization of America, chairman of the United Jewish War Effort, chairman of the American Jewish Conference, and cochairman of the Commission of Rescue of the American Jewish Conference.[17]

Rabbi Wise did not procrastinate two or three days when he received the pleas from Massena at the end of September. Immediately, on September 28, Bernard Richards, executive secretary of the American Jewish

Congress, ripped off a telegram to Jake Shulkin that read:

DR WISE HAS WRITTEN   PLEASE ACKNOWL-
EDGE   FORWARD ANY SUGGESTION FUR-
THER STEPS   URGE YOU DEMAND FORMAL
APOLOGY ALSO SECURE NAME SOCALLED FOR-
EIGNER RESPONSIBLE SPREADING OUTRA-
GEOUS RUMOR [18]

Wise had indeed authorized a communiqué to Shulkin expressing "pain and shock" at the intimations of ritual murder. He declared that the matter must be cleared up immediately, with "an unequivocal apology." [19] As proof that he did not propose to let the matter rest, on September 29, three days before Louis Marshall was moved to action, Wise directed additional letters to Major Warner, Mayor Hawes, and Joseph Ellis of Watertown, New York. The last missive, intended for a Zionist contact, was sent for the purpose of having the reliable Ellis make a separate, confidential report on conditions in Massena, 70 miles away from Watertown. That particular correspondence was, however, of little importance.[20]

More interesting was Wise's letter to Warner. Though the rabbi knew Governor Smith's son-in-law well enough to call him by name, this note was unusually formal. Wise found it difficult "to bring a very painful and even humiliating matter" to Warner's attention. Despite such sensitivity, he was constrained to ask "that action be taken without a moment's delay." And here he explained to the state's highest-ranking police officer what had occurred at Massena and how public officials had momentarily supported the charge that Jews used human blood for their High Holy Day services.

"I dare say," Wise went on, "that you have heard that these hideous and ghastly rumors of 'ritual murder' float about in East European lands in order that excuse may be found for wrong done to Jews. I know that you will feel as I do that the fullest amends must be made to the Jewish community of Massena and that nothing less than a most explicit apology will be satisfactory.

"I take it for granted," Wise concluded, "that you will send for the Trooper, secure the fullest statement from him in the matter and see to it that such action follows as will make clear to the citizenship of Massena that this awful charge is completely and contritely withdrawn as far as the member of the State Troop is concerned." [21]

With Mayor Hawes, Wise was more abrupt. First, he took note of the attempted resurrection of what he termed "this ancient and unspeakable libel" and the role of Trooper McCann and Hawes in questioning Rabbi Brennglass. "I trust that for your sake that story is not true and that you will find it possible to deny it," he wrote. "Taking it for granted, as I do, that you desire as far as possible to repair the hurt that has been done, I most earnestly suggest to you that you do whatever may be necessary not merely to contradict the base rumour of ritual murder, but point out in addition that no intelligent, decent person has ever given any credence to this charge which has been exposed, whenever made, wherever made, and laid to rest time and again by the heads of the Christian churches." Wise concluded with a demand for a full statement from Hawes concerning his involvement in the affair. The rabbi omitted his customary friendly salutation.[22]

Privately, to Bernard Richards, Wise expressed the hope that his three letters would suffice. "Warner I know," he said in a memorandum dated September 28, "and I thought that if I don't immediately get satisfaction from the Mayor I will have charges placed against him to the Governor. The Governor can remove a Mayor. We would, of course, have to wait until after the election." [23]

Over the weekend, though, Wise must have changed his mind and decided that pressure should be applied to Smith. On Tuesday, October 2, the same day Marshall was uttering declamations to the press, Wise phoned the state capital and apprised Smith directly of what had happened. The governor responded as Wise knew he would. Smith's only declaration on the incident at Massena was read by his assistant Belle Moskowitz over the phone to the American Jewish Congress on Wednesday morning, October 3, before being released (with some modifications) to the press that same day. Significantly, it was addressed to Rabbi Wise and read:

> Dear Dr. Wise:
> I had not heard before this hour when your message reached me of the rumour of ritual murder which developed on Jewish Atonement Day at Massena, St. Lawrence County.
> As Governor of the State, I cannot believe that this libelous myth has been resurrected and credited even for a moment by any one connected with the service of the State, or any of its civil divisions. I can hardly believe that either the Mayor of Massena or a State

Trooper summoned a rabbi to a police station on a
religious holiday in connection with an absurd ritual
murder charge to account for the disappearance of a
child, which, I learned, was found again within a few
hours of its disappearance.

I wish to assure you that I will see to it as the
Governor of the State of New York that this matter
be investigated in the most thorough manner as to
the action of the State Trooper. I have, however, no
control over the mayors of villages. The public officers law provides means of making charges against
them.

Sincerely yours,
Alfred E. Smith [24]

It is interesting to note that major surgery was performed on the last paragraph of this letter between the
time it was read to the American Jewish Congress and
the time it appeared in the *New York Times*. In the
original version, Smith privately promised investigation
"without one moment's delay." Further, he warned: "If
the Mayor of Massena be responsible for this charge,
the Law Department of the State will take such action
as is necessary." In a mood of honest anger that apparently must not be allowed public servants, Smith added:
"There will be no toleration of an attempt by any public
official to give countenance to the grotesque accusation
of ritual murder, or any equally baseless indictment
against a whole people by the citizenship of America, at
least not in this State, while I am its Governor." [25]
These courageous words, as valid as anything Smith
had uttered in Oklahoma City two weeks before, never
reached print.

In any event, it was Wise, then, not Louis Marshall,
who first brought the matter to the attention of state

authorities. This would prove telling in the further disposition of the case. But it was Marshall who capitalized on the coincidental appearance of his own letter in the press on October 2 and Smith's letter the following day. It was Marshall who seized upon the potential celebrity of the case, proclaiming himself the champion of the Jewish people against this libel. Such action cannot, however, be attributed solely to Marshall's penchant for grandstanding.

Men of Marshall's prestige, Stephen Wise included, have succumbed at one time or another to a form of self-mesmerism. Surrounded by fawning subordinates, privy to some processes affecting social and political life, they view themselves with inflated importance. Marshall was such a man—self-important, vain, and jealous. He did not like Wise, nor did he especially trust him. It was significant for Marshall (a Republican) that Wise, a lifelong Democrat and a close associate of Al Smith since the disastrous Triangle Shirtwaist Fire of 1911, just might attempt to distort the issue out of its true nature and convert it into a campaign issue in that tempestuous election year. The governor, surrounded as he was by Jewish advisers such as Abram Elkus, Bernard Shientag, Joseph Proskauer, Samuel Untermeyer, Jesse Straus, Aaron Levy, Clarence Stein, Herbert Lehman, Aaron Rabinowitz, and Michael Friedsam, and aware of the political clout of New York State's 2,000,000 Jews, just might be receptive to such an issue, especially since Republicans happened to be the villains. It would be up to Marshall to keep the case in its true perspective and not let anyone profiteer at the expense of the Jews.[26]

Marshall did Al Smith a disservice if he suggested, even for a moment, that the governor might make political fodder of the incident. While it was true he could become the chief beneficiary of a political fight over Massena, it was equally true that Al Smith was a man possessing keen sensitivity toward human suffering. A mixture of Italian, German, English, and Irish ancestry, Smith had known poverty and bigotry growing up in New York's Fourth Ward. His grandparents, Irish immigrants, arrived in this country in 1841, just at the beginning of the Know Nothing hysteria. His mother was widowed and had to work to keep her six children in school. From the Bowery to Delancey and Grand Streets, one could find families of Germans, Italians, Hispanic-Americans, Chinese, and Russian Jews crowded into brownstone tenements. And all with the common goal of surviving and having a better life one day.

Smith did not pander to these people with the hope of winning their votes in the upcoming election. Some experts, noting massive upstate registration, usually indicative of a heavy Republican turnout, had already written off his home state.[27] Nor was he pressured by the few letters he received from Little Rock, Arkansas; Columbus, Ohio; Mountain View, New York; or Washington, D.C.[28] Rather, he was guided by what his father had said when he intervened to save a couple of blacks during the draft riots of July 1863: "They are children of God and have a right to live." [29] Smith would have no further official comment on the incident of Massena.

Jews could be buoyed by Smith's promise of a complete inquiry at the state capital. The fact that Major

Warner, who already had released Lieutenant Heim's report to the press, would be conducting the investigation was encouraging. There were some rumblings, however, about a separate legislative investigation at the insistence of Assemblyman Julius Berg, head of the Jewish Veterans of the Wars of the Republic. Berg had wired Mayor Hawes on October 2, threatening to institute proceedings for his removal unless he resigned.[30] That action was prompted by something that seemed to erase all cause for optimism: a letter from the mayor to Rabbi Wise, also dated Tuesday, October 2, 1928.

Asked to recant his role in the incident, Hawes replied with hauteur. He explained that he had discussed the matter with "a committee representing the local Jewish organization" and "a Mr. B. Smolar of the Jewish branch of Associated Press." "The incident has been enlarged and magnified," Hawes wrote, "and from the contents of your letter I feel sure that you do not fully understand the facts." The man who at that very moment was spearheading an economic boycott of Jewish businesses in Massena continued: "I regret exceedingly that this misunderstanding has arisen. I hold no ill feeling against the Jewish people of this community and I know that there is no local prejudice or hostility. Our community has been cooperating in a common civic and industrial endeavor here and I hope that the exceedingly pleasant relations which have prevailed here in the past may continue without interruption. If I am chargeable with any act or word in this matter which has been offensive to the Jewish people, I certainly regret it." [31]

Wise was not satisfied by the mayor's cryptic note,

which he indicated was "too vague to constitute an apology." [32] The tone of the letter was almost flippant, as if Hawes did not recognize that any harm had been done. Nor was Wise deceived by Hawes's contention that most Massenans were ignorant of the affair. How, then, to explain the hundreds of people who had materialized before City Hall and Adath Israel on Sunday, September 23? Nor was Wise cowed by the thinly veiled threat against the welfare of Massena's Jewish population should publicity continue to mount in the direction of the North Country. Something more substantial had to be forthcoming from Hawes, or legal action against the mayor would be mandatory.

In Massena, Mayor Hawes feigned imperturbability, but it was impossible for him to ignore the practically universal adverse criticism. The Massena libel was bannered across the nation, as Louis Marshall and Stephen Wise had calculated. Parts of Marshall's letter were even cited in the October 3 issue of the *London Times.* [33] In New York, the *Herald-Tribune, World, Sun, Times, Post, Brooklyn Eagle,* and *Daily News* all reacted with controlled outrage. Typical was the *Sun,* a paper until then not especially known for catering to Jewish readers. Its editorial of October 4, headed "Stamp Out This Fire!" went on to say:

> Somewhere in the blackest abyss of the Dark Ages, malice and stupidity continued to invent this slander against the Jews. They were accused of murdering Christian children, using their blood in sacrificial rites. So far as anybody has been able to ascertain, there never has been a Jewish ritualistic practice

which gave even the slightest color of plausibility to this hoary lie. But it has been revived from time to time among superstitious peasants in the most backward parts of Europe, serving to inflame them to anti-Semitic rage and incite them to pogroms. Until now, however, American common sense has prevented this grotesque libel from gaining credence here. This kind of thing is like fire in stubble, easily stamped out at first, but hard to control once it gains headway.[34]

The *Louisville Courier-Journal,* commenting on the affair, noted with rectitude: "Such an inquisition couldn't have taken place in America. The next impulse is to look at the name of the town again. The thing didn't happen in the South. If it had, the entire populace would have been indicted for the single isolated instance of barbarity." [35] Nearer to home, correspondents for the *Syracuse Post-Standard* and *Watertown Times* churned out stories that left little doubt that Mayor Hawes was the man responsible for the incident and that the people of Massena were a collection of Mesozoic muffs.

The only journal that totally ignored the racial-religious angle in the story was the *Massena Observer.* Its sole article on the disappearance of Barbara Griffiths came in the September 27 issue and did not mention the anti-Jewish trouble in town that week. The closest that editor L. C. Sutton ever came to assessing the case was an editorial on November 8, titled "Considering Massena." Amid *sboyet* worthy of Hugh Hefner, cautioning Massena not to become a boomtown "like New York or London," Sutton unintentionally put his finger on the ugly mood in Massena that fall. "Let us be sure," he wrote, "that Massena does not go mad in the pursuit of strange gods. Let us use common sense to understand the exact place of Massena in the scheme of things." [36]

W. Gilbert Hawes appreciated Sutton's silence, for he needed all the friends he could find. The mayor was under severe pressure from a quarter other than the press. Each day since the publication of Marshall's letter, another shipment of denunciatory mail had arrived, some of it containing resolutions passed by Jewish congregations in Baltimore, San Francisco, or Cincinnati, other pieces of hate mail that referred to Hawes as a "son of a bitch" or "bastard" and promised "We'll kill you" or simply "We will come up and get you." Seward Hanmer remembers stacks of what he terms vicious, nasty letters and three-foot-long telegrams from Jews around the country that "scared the mayor to death." [37]

Persons under mental siege become somewhat paranoid about the telephone, and Hawes was no exception. He maintained that he was being harassed on the line, that people were listening in on his conversations (though it seems impossible that any Jew in Massena would have dared such activity at the time). Things were so bad for the mayor during that first week of October that he requested and received special police protection around the clock at his home. Eli Friedman and Saul Rosenbaum, both of whom lived around the corner from the Hawes house on Andrews Avenue, once took a late-evening stroll into town. They noticed something glistening on the lawn before the big stone home. As the object moved into the streetlight, they recognized the leather puttees of a state trooper who was on duty at the mayor's home. In a town where the boycott of Jewish stores did not end until the mayor himself loudly ballyhooed that he was trading with the Shulkins and Stones and Kauffmans, the trooper remained on duty for nearly a month.[38]

Hawes was frightened by his sudden notoriety and did not relish tilting with giants like Smith, Marshall, or Wise. Many times since September 22–23, he wished he had just kept his mouth shut and stayed out of the picture, as Chief San Jule had done. Like a chastened puppy, he had followed the advice of attorney Hanmer, apologizing to the Jewish leaders in town, apologizing directly to Rabbi Brennglass, and even writing to Rabbi Wise and the Jewish papers in New York, but none of this had sufficed. When Wise announced the mayor's apology was insufficient, newsmen from the wire services sought out Hawes for additional comment. The mayor was unavailable, but attorney Hanmer intervened once more in an effort to rescue his hapless colleague.

In a special press conference held on October 3, Andrew Hanmer went over the incident again in detail, conceding that Hawes had been the instigator of the questioning of Rabbi Brennglass. He declared, however, that the mayor had apologized to all principals and that his apology was a sincere one. Those who rejected it "had misconstrued the entire affair and had circulated a wrong impression of the mayor's attitude." As for Louis Marshall's letter, Hanmer stated that up to 10:00 P.M. the previous night, the mayor had received no letter from Marshall and that both he and Hanmer had learned of the interest of the American Jewish Committee's president only from the morning's newspapers.

When queried as to what might now be expected, Hanmer hedged, indicating that the next move was not up to the mayor. He had done all that any reasonable man could do. It was now up to the Jewish community either to let the thing die down or to continue to malign and persecute a man who had conceded the error of his ways. Asked what effect the governor's statement might make in the case, Hanmer could not guess, although he did grant that Corporal McCann, whose term in Massena had ended abruptly with the publication of the Marshall letter (and whose departure was never noted by the *Massena Observer,* which had so graciously welcomed him to town a month before), almost certainly would be reprimanded. Would he, Hanmer, go to Albany to see Smith or Major Warner concerning the incident? The village attorney smiled and said he did not know. Later that same day, the Associated Press reported that Hanmer was en route to Albany. The purpose of his trip was not yet known.[39]

13

*L*ouis Marshall reached the offices of the
American Jewish Committee at 171 Madison Avenue in
New York shortly after 10:00 A.M. on Thursday, October 4. He was expecting two very important visitors
from Massena later that day: Joseph Stone and J. J.
Kauffman. The machinery he had set in motion by
dispatching Boris Smolar upstate was now beginning to
pick up speed. On the heels of his published letter,
Marshall had sent a telegram to the Adath Israel congregation, requesting more information and promising
to render all legal, financial, and moral support of the
Committee to the Jews in Massena. This very day, the
mail would bring a letter from Major Warner (identical
to one sent Rabbi Wise) acknowledging Marshall's
interest in the affair. Warner "heartily deplored" the
incident and promised prompt action to rectify the situation.[1] An unpacified Marshall, ever conscious of his

role in this drama, was already mapping a multilateral legal assault on Hawes, McCann, and several others in Massena.

Unfortunately for Marshall, however, the main theater for the drama was not to be in New York, or even, for that matter, in Massena. During his session with Stone and Kauffman, a secretary entered Marshall's office, bearing a telegram. From Eli Friedman, it indicated that Stone was to drop everything and rush north to Albany if possible.[2] Major Warner had called a special meeting in the capital for that very day. Jake Shulkin, Berel Brennglass, McCann, Hawes and Hanmer were on their way from Massena, and a delegation of Marshall's rivals from the American Jewish Congress, including Rabbi Wise, Bernard Richards, Louis Lande, and attorney George Gordon Battle,[3] were meeting with Warner, Heim, and Captain James Broadfield of the State Police.

Marshall's rage at being slighted, ignored in an incident over which he claimed proprietary rights, was for the moment controlled when Stone explained that the whole thing had caught them by surprise. Why else would Stone and Kauffman, the leading spokesmen of Massena's Jews, have come all the way to New York?[4] The men sat with Marshall, feeling embarrassed and impotent.

The meeting in Albany was held behind closed doors in the executive chambers of the capitol building. No notes or minutes of this "exhaustive hearing"[5] survive. But based on references in letters from Warner to Wise and Marshall we may surmise that it proceeded along certain lines.

Warner opened the stiffly formal hearing with a statement from Governor Smith expressing his concern about the gravity of the affair and Smith's feeling that its importance should not be minimized. (Had the governor been in attendance himself, the language would have been more earthy.) Heim's optimistic report was also reviewed, with dissents from the Massena delegation and with Rabbi Wise stressing the historic villainy of the ritual-murder charge. Mayor Hawes's position was rationalized somewhat unhappily by his counsel, Hanmer. And the mayor offered a timorous statement on his own behalf.[6]

When it was over after three hours and the group walked out, newsmen from all the major wire services, New York papers, and upstate press who had clustered about the second floor of the Renaissance monstrosity on State Street for most of the morning were on hand to accept statements. Typically, the reporting, even of the venerable *New York Times,* was defective. (The *Times* noted the presence of *William* Shulkin, Jake's boy, as the president of the Jewish congregation of Massena, and referred to Rabbi Brennglass with a variety of exotic spellings that week.) [7] About the only accurate stories related to prepared statements distributed by Hawes and McCann to the press.

With unexpected eloquence, Hawes declared:

> I am confirmed in my conviction that I have committed a serious error of judgment into which I was led in part by the excitement incident to the disappearance of the Griffiths' child of my community. In

the light of what I have learned since the incident and particularly in the light of the solemn protest of my Jewish neighbors, I feel that I ought to express clearly and unequivocally as I now do, my deep and sincere regret that by any act of commission or omission, I should have seemed to lend countenance even for a moment to what I ought to have known to be a cruel libel imputing human sacrifice as a practice now or at any time in the history of the Jewish people.

I clearly see and I have no hesitation in affirming that when first the suggestion was made that the disappearance of the Griffiths child might be associated with the alleged practice of human sacrifice by the Jews, far from giving hospitable ear to the suggestion, I should have repelled it with indignation and advised the state trooper to desist from his intention of making inquiry of the respected rabbi of the Jewish community of Massena concerning a rumor so monstrous and fantastic.

I should have known what I did not know but since have learned, that in the Middle Ages Jews have paid an awful toll in life because of just such unthinkable charges and that the accusation of ritual murder was imputed, in the early Christian centuries, by pagan peoples to the disciples of the Christian churches.

I now see that I was no more jusitfied in permitting the rabbi of the Congregation of Massena, representing the ancient and honorable congregation of Israel, to be interrogated with regard to the myth of ritual murder than I would have been justified in permitting the minister of any Protestant church or the bishop of the Catholic diocese including Massena to be questioned concerning ritual murder as a Christian church practice if the person under wrongful suspicion, as was this Jewish boy, had chanced to be a member of any one of the Christian communions.

> I write this word of heartfelt apology because I would do justice not only to the Jewish people of Massena, but because I desire to offer complete and unreserved amends to that great people which has given to the world the God which I worship and the religion I love.
>
> I do not make this statement of profound regret because of any fear on my part that charges will be brought against me looking to my removal from the office of Mayor, to which I have been elected five times, four of these times being unanimous. I know that the citizens of Massena, including its Jewish members, will not seek to dishonor me through removal from office because of an error in judgment which no one deplores more than I do.[8]

The apology was better constructed than Hawes's earlier statement to Wise, but implicit in it, just as in the former, was a tone of insincerity, of Hawes's being the unwitting accomplice of a state trooper (McCann) who had insisted on interrogating "the respected rabbi." McCann's statement was simpler and undoubtedly sincere. To Rabbi Brennglass, he wrote: "I regret more than I can tell you, and am very, very sorry for my part in the incident at Massena. After the hearing today, I realize as I did not before, how wrong it was of me to request you to come to the police station at Massena to be questioned concerning a rumor which I should have known to be absolutely false. I was terribly excited and fatigued at the time, having been on duty for many hours without food or rest. Otherwise I would have thought of the consequence of such an act and would not have done what I did. I mean every word of this apology and I hope you will take it in the spirit in which it is written." [9]

In a sense, McCann was to be the fall guy for the affair. He was given an indefinite suspension "for gross lack of discretion in the exercise of his duties and for conduct most unbecoming an officer" [10] and was transferred away from Saint Lawrence County. After more than twenty years in the service, during which time he never rose above the rank of corporal, he retired from the State Police without ever commenting further in public about the matter.

When Louis Marshall picked up his morning *Times* on October 5 and read the little article on page 27 titled "Mayor of Massena Makes an Apology," he was livid. That same day, he dictated a blistering letter to Major Warner, demanding to know why "for some inexplicable reason" he (Marshall) had not been apprised of the Albany meeting. Why hadn't *his* witnesses (and here the president of the American Jewish Committee appropriated Stone and Kauffman as personal property) been called, when they possessed vital information on the "wanton outrage against all Jews?" Marshall also waved aside Lieutenant Heim's report, calling it inadequate and insisting that the incident be further probed.[11]

"My criticism," Marshall concluded, "is of the extraordinary manner in which this proceeding was rushed through immediately upon the heels of the publication of my letter which indicated the enormity of the offense committed. While I do not pretend to be a great mathematician, I am at least able to appreciate that 2 plus 2 make 4. If you desire an explanation of this cryptic statement, I can give it to you." [12]

Warner sought no explication, but Marshall subsequently clarified what he meant in another angry letter to Rabbi Brennglass. Here he charged "there was an attempt to bring the matter into partisan politics and for that reason the gentlemen who went to Albany from here thought it desirable that I should be kept in ignorance of what was going on." [13] In other words, the Democratic Party machine, with its American Jewish Congress lackeys, was trying to exploit the affair for political gain. They would not care for the presence of a moderate or neutral Jewish representative like Marshall at Albany.

The best comeback to this unfounded charge was contained in a letter to Rabbi Wise from an old crony, Morris Margulies, on October 8. Wrote Margulies: "An old but none the less constant admirer sends congratulations on the fine and successful method pursued in connection with the Massina]sic] affair. After this *his Majesty Louis the Somewhat)* [italics mine] ought to be more careful in writing long legalistic letters in a State where 'Al' is His Excellency the Governor." [14]

Marshall's rage in those next few days of October ran unchecked. The same day Hawes's letter of apology was printed (October 5), he wrote the major an acknowledgment on behalf of the Jewish people (even though Hawes had not addressed his statement to Marshall). Still, Marshall insisted that the published apology was inadequate. He wanted yet another public statement "in terms more appropriate for the occasion," and even took the liberty of enclosing a draft for Hawes to sign and return.[15] No copies of this document are extant. Hawes, fed up with all Jewish groups, probably destroyed it.

Marshall felt betrayed, left out, like a child whose
parents had reneged on a trip to the zoo. He reacted
accordingly—with intellectual tantrums. When Shulkin
and Brennglass tried to inform him of what had happened at Albany, telling him that the Jews of Massena
were entirely satisfied with the sincerity of the apologies, that they wanted to live in peace with their Christian neighbors, and that they felt the best disposition for
the incident was to consider it closed, [16] Marshall ex-
ploded again.

A return letter to Shulkin, dated October 6, began
with a moderate tone, expressing "surprise" that Marshall had not been invited to the Albany hearing, especially since the Jews of Massena had solicited American Jewish Committee assistance first, and since Marshall had electrified the nation with his public letter.
How could Shulkin and Brennglass have permitted the
charade to take place in Albany at the very moment
their close friends Joe Stone and Jesse Kauffman were
in New York City? Why had they failed to tell others
that they had been summoned to the office of the superintendent of the State Police that Thursday? Weren't
the telephones that had roused Marshall from the tran-
quillity of his bedchamber on the night of September 22
still operating?

Then Marshall really lost his temper. In "fifty years of
Jewish activity," he said, he had never received a letter
like the one that Shulkin and Brennglass had written
calling for an end to the affair. Marshall protested "the
most cavalier manner [which] practically dismisses me
from the case and decides *an important proposition
which in no manner concerns you* [italics mine], that is

the attitude of the Jewish people as a whole to the case." [17] Here was Louis Marshall, New York patrician, telling Massena's Jews, the people who had lived through a night of terror and were still trying to cope with a boycott and continued intimidation from the Ku Klux Klan, that the "proposition" did not concern them.

Marshall went on to say that he was not satisfied with Hawes's apology because it sounded too much "like a lecture and is utterly devoid of sincerity." He may have been correct on both counts. The statement may have been the product of a collaboration between Rabbi Wise and attorney Hanmer. Whatever the case, Marshall noted that Hawes's closing paragraph was couched in phrases that should be most offensive to a self-respecting Jew, especially when such an expression came from a man who only a week before had been "guilty of the most serious offense ever perpetrated in this country upon the Jewish people, infinitely worse than anything that Henry Ford ever did." [18]

It seemed as if everyone in the country had been placated by Hawes's apology but Marshall. The *New York World* considered the statement "adequate" and added that it "should put an end to a deplorable incident." [19] The *American Hebrew* also expressed satisfaction with the retraction and reprimand, and stated that "any further pressure exercised by American Jews would savor of vindictiveness." [20] With strained eloquence, Barry O'Neil of the little-known *Nation Wide Review* preached: "Let us meet the Jew as a business man in this United States. Or if one wishes, as a man of another race. Yet primarily, let us meet the Jew . . . as a

man!" [21] Even the daily Yiddish press was mollified, as
the *Morning Journal* and *Der Tog* bannered triumphant
stories of the events in Albany, replete with pictures of
attorney George Battle.[22]

From their pulpits in New York City, Rabbis Herbert
Goldstein and Jacob Katz praised the swiftness and
severity of the treatment that had been meted out, but
prayed for leniency and understanding. And a statement issued by the Permanent Commission on Better
Understanding between Christians and Jews, chaired by
Dr. W. H. P. Faunce, president of Brown University,
and including such notables as Roscoe Pound, dean of
the Harvard Law School, Reverend Franics Duffy, president of the Rainbow Division of the Veterans Association, Reverend S. Parkes Cadman, president of the
Federal Council of Churches of Christ in America, Justice Victor Dowling of the New York Appellate Division, Martin Conboy, knight commander of the Order
of Saint Gregory the Great, Judge Irving Lehman of the
State Court of Appeals, and Henry Morgenthau, Sr.,
former ambassador to Turkey, also condemned the "abhorrent fiction" and praised authorities for bringing the
issue to a close.[23]

On October 9, Marshall received a wire from Julius
Frank, the Jewish mayor of Ogdensburg, asking him to
cease pressure on Massena. Frank indicated he had
conferred with Jake Shulkin, Joe Stone, and Simon
Levine, and they had concluded that further publicity
"will seriously affect the future welfare of the Jewish
residents not alone of Massena, but of all the North
Country." [24] The confidence and spirit of the Jews had
progressively eroded with the continuation of the eco-

nomic boycott, minor incidents on the streets and fights in the schools, and a general feeling of distemper rampant in Massena as a result of the public degradation of one of their own citizens, their titular leader. After three weeks of tension, during which Roy and Willard Countryman and their fire station followers had remained belligerent, the Jews were anxious to purchase peace at the cost of silence. They also requested that Assemblyman Berg go no further in his efforts to make a legislative inquiry into the matter or bring charges against Hawes before the State Supreme Court.[25]

It was a far cry from the courageous responses of September 22–23, when Massena's Jews had stood up without any official support. But it was a more understandable position than that which Marshall displayed. His response to this wire demonstrated that concern for the welfare of the people of Massena or the honor of the Jewish people in general had somehow been transmuted into a question of *personal* honor. He replied to Frank that he had no intention of jeopardizing the Jews of upper New York State, but he wanted an apology from Hawes, a genuine apology, addressed *to him*.[26]

Marshall's public stance as vicar of the Jewish people, his monomania concerning another apology, prompted Rabbi Brennglass to write him again asking that he desist from his actions allegedly on behalf of Massena's Jews.[27] Marshall wrote back (on October 20) that he was not attempting to create unpleasantness for the Jews in town, but he resented the effort to make the issue a political one, to keep him in the dark, and to readily accept Hawes's letter, which, he said, "sounds cheaply rhetorical and makes Mr. Hawes appear like a

great moralist instead of the ignoramus that he is." [28]
Marshall believed that Hawes had refused to sign his
(Marshall's) confession because someone else had told
him not to. Knowing Hawes' relationship with attorney
Hanmer, there is every likelihood that this was so. But if
Marshall believed he could bully or intimidate Hawes
into another statement, he was mistaken. The only communiqué he ever received from the mayor included a
copy of Hawes's statement to Rabbi Wise with the nota-
tion "I assume that this statement fully covers the incident and is in keeping with the spirit of the suggestions
made to me in your communication of October 1st." [29]

By November 10, 1928, Marshall had calmed down
sufficiently to offer ten minutes on the subject of Massena before the executive committee of the American
Jewish Committee. There was no mention of the mayor,
however, except to note his public apology, the same
apology Marshall had rejected.[30]

Later that month, the American Jewish Congress
under Rabbi Wise would host a delegation from Massena at its convention in Atlantic City. The honored
guests included Rabbi Brennglass (who delivered a
short address to the convention), Joseph Stone, J. J.
Kauffman, and Jake Shulkin.[31] At no time during this
meeting or in subsequent writings did Rabbi Wise al-
lude to the personality clash with Louis Marshall that
had sullied this triumph for all Jews. Biographies of the
leader of the American Jewish Committee are equally
silent on the subject.[32]

The Yiddish daily *Der Tog*, in summing up the case
on October 6, noted "the fact that the story begins with

Marshall and ends with Wise makes and must make an unpleasant impression." The editors expressed doubt whether Marshall would be satisfied with the published apology or demand another. What was tragic throughout this incident in their eyes, however, was that petty jealousy and enmity, divisions that had surfaced, even momentarily, within the Jewish organizations, had pushed the peril faced by Massena's Jews into the background. According to *Der Tog:* "It certainly is an abnormal state of affairs that American Jewry is doomed to a double representation. It is not only abnormal, but also unhealthy for the entire body of American Jewry. The symptoms of this unhealthy state of affairs come to the fore at avarious occasions when community problems have to be solved in various degrees of imitation." [33]

What happened in 1928 between the two principal Jewish groups and their leaders presaged future events: the anomie and friction, the backbiting and conniving that would deprive American Jewry of effective action during the Holocaust. Egotism and divisiveness would not contribute to the saving of 6,000,000 Jews, because Eric and James Warburg would counsel President Franklin D. Roosevelt against immigration relief for German Jews in 1933; because Rabbi Wise and Baruch Vladeck of the Jewish Labor Committee would not be able to agree over tactics for the boycott of Nazi goods in 1937; because Wise and other leaders would never be able to mount a unified response to the bloody *Kristallnacht* pogrom of 1938; because leaders of the American Jewish Congress, the American Jewish Committee, B'nai B'rith, and the Jewish Labor Committee would not renounce personal prestige to assure the success of the General Jewish Council (which was intended to be an umbrella organization for all Jews in the United States, but which died an unlamented death in 1941); because Wise would not allow the validity of any schemes suggested by the Revisionist New Zionist Organization of America, the Committee for an Army of Stateless and Palestinian Jews, or the Emergency Conference to Save the Jews of Europe, even when such schemes could have saved lives during World War II; because assimilationist elements of the American Jewish Committee would not countenance a plan like the 1942 Biltmore Program, calling for a Jewish state in Palestine, and walked out to establish their own self-hating claque, the American Council for Judaism.[34]

The shades of the tragedy that was to befall Europe's Jews, the ineptitude and *obstanovotchka* (a term used by Vladimir Jabotinsky to describe a tendency on the part of many Jews to myopia, narrowmindedness, or thinking small) of American Jews were all contained in the aftermath of the incident at Massena.

14

Today, Massena, New York, is a bustling community of 16,000 people, still a mélange of nationalities and religions, but no longer Republican. A modern radio station, housed in one of the several first-class motels that cater to Saint Lawrence Seaway tourism, plays the latest in rock and roll. A new state arterial highway slithers out to the Eisenhower Locks, where one can gape at huge oceangoing ore boats that plod on from the Midwest. The old Nightingale Section has become Windsor, Cedar Hill, Sherwood, Kirkland, and a host of other streets with lovely homes and a modern school complex. The State Police are now housed in their own white saltbox on East Orvis Street and rarely disturb anyone but unsuspecting speeders in the vicinity of Morristown. And Massena's police chief, a handsome, bright, stocky young man named Dale Wright, bears not the faintest resemblance either in methodology or intellect to his predecessors.

Stephen Wise, Louis Marshall, John Warner, and Al Smith are all dead. Marshall's fears that the "Happy Warrior" might try to exploit the incident for political gain proved baseless. Most newspapers, including the Jewish press, let the matter die after the first week of October, and Smith never did make reference to it in the last weeks of the Presidential campaign. Silently, he waged his fight for tolerance, and the result was defeat, not merely for the Presidency but even in his own state. Herbert Hoover carried New York that November by a margin of 2,913,344 votes to 2,089,863. Smith never lived to see his son-in-law, Major Warner, revert to the GOP and support Thomas E. Dewey between dalliances as guest soloist with orchestras in Rochester, Cleveland, Boston, and New York's Radio City Music Hall.

Gone, too, are Rabbi Brennglass, Jake Shulkin, Joe Stone, J. J. Kauffman, Andrew Hanmer, Morris Goldberg, W. Gilbert Hawes, and Mickey McCann. Some of their homes may yet be seen in Massena, their businesses, too, and friends and relatives. Hawes was able to cling to the mayorship for another two years, but with defeat at the hands of a Democrat in 1931, his standing in the community evaporated. Deserted by his first wife, despondent and broken in health, he died in 1948, something of an anachronism.

Dave and Marion Griffiths still live on Cherry Street in a little home of their own. The memory of the incident has never faded from their thoughts. Marion

THE INCIDENT AT MASSENA

Griffiths lost the child she was carrying in 1928. Fortunately, their daughter, Barbara, suffered no trauma from the experience, no fear of the outdoors. She grew up, married, moved to Canton, and has reared three children of her own. In one of the touching ironies of this sad story, her youngest boy, Mike Klemens, a 1971 graduate of Dartmouth, spent one summer working with retarded girls at Sunmouth in Tupper Lake and indicated a desire to make work with the mentally handicapped his life's vocation.

The true victim in the affair, Willie Shulkin, lives today with his wife in Rochester, New York. Handicapped by a condition few in town cared to understand, he remembers nothing of what happened that weekend in September 1928. And yet he had to endure years of derision, the stigma of being "the Shulkin boy." With the help of the courageous young woman from Syracuse whom he married, Willie carved out a new life and reared a child who is bright, beautiful, and devoted to her parents.

It is not my purpose to engage in a long dissertation on mental health. Every town has its own strange people. The white-haired kid in Berea, Ohio, who sits on a bench at the Triangle, grinning and making knots while waiting for the Route A bus. The harmless sixty-year-old Jew in Boardman, Ohio, who hitchhikes rides and is an embarrassment to his congregation. The retarded children who want to live out in the community, mingle at petting zoos, or see Santa. The deaf man in Peekskill, New York, whose efforts at speech are lost upon an intolerant small merchant. The skid-row derelicts who gain a moment of notoriety at Salvation Army tables every Christmas. In a sense, Willie Shulkin represents them all—all "different," "queer," "crazy"—and yet none of these things. An intolerant society needs to learn that patience and understanding go a long way with such people, that like Willie Shulkin they can make lives for themselves, be loving and capable parents. Our society has a long way to go before the words of Al Smith's father ring true: "They are children of God and have a right to live."

Today, few people in Massena under the age of sixty know anything about the affair that stained the town's honor in 1928. It would be nice to report that Massena, like the rest of the nation, took to heart the instruction of Rabbi Wise, who wrote:

> The lesson of Massena is for all Americans. The way to banish religious intolerance and bigotry and all their hateful consequences is to be firm and resolute against everything that savors of injustice between faith and faith, people and people. The ritual murder myth is only a little more obvious and monstrous than other myths in the realm of religious divisions. Americans must always mean the most eager passion to do justice as well as to obtain it. The Massena incident is now closed—happily for Israelism and Christendom. Christianity must see to it that it never again be revived on the soil of America.[1]

In the fifty years since Barbara Griffiths wandered into the woods, there have been few anti-Semitic incidents in Massena. The Jews in town were not bothered during the first week of October 1928 when two orphan boys, Joel and Ray Orcott, disappeared into the woods and were gone nearly two weeks [2] (something that belies the popular contention among old-timers that the disappearance of the Griffiths child was the only such occurrence in the town's history). Nor were Jews of the North Country singled out in 1954 when a three-year-old child from the village of Duane, some 30 miles away, disappeared for three days and was recovered after having spent the time in the hillocks leading to the Adirondacks.[3] Nor was there any special anti-Jewish significance to the leaflet posted on the bulletin board of Massena's renovated police offices warning children against molesters.[4]

And yet it would be simplistic to suggest that the situation for Jews in this small town is idyllic today. Despite the obvious involvent of the Ku Klux Klan in the 1928 incident, neither the Countrymans nor Comnas were ever pressed for an apology. Despite the fact that a number of Jews had served in World War I (many were members of the American Legion), that more served in World War II (including Leonard Cohen, who lost his life in the Battle of the Bulge),[5] no Jews were allowed in the Monday Luncheon Club of Massena until the 1960s.[6] Despite a shrinking Jewish population, which could not even afford a full-time rabbi after 1965, and which certainly posed no menace to the community, Adath Israel was desecrated during the swastika-smearing epidemic of 1959–1960. Abby "Al" Slavin, son of Sam Slavin, was forced to organize a volunteer patrol of the synagogue grounds every half hour.[7] And Seward Hanmer reports, "Recently, when a kid drowned in the river, the cellars of the stores downtown were searched. It was hoped that he might have gone in."[8]

Before 1928, and since, there was never another full-blown charge of ritual murder against the Jews in the United States. And yet one must wonder, as I did when I visited Massena, if that record is something to be proud of. In talking with one of the best-educated men in town, a man with a college education and great prestige in the community, I was told of the charge that Jews used blood: *"It was a false rumor, for all I know* [italics mine]." He was not the only Gentile in Massena who expressed "doubts" about the ritual-murder canard. When I discussed the nature of the charge with two others, I was dumbstruck by the simple question: "Well, do they? Do the Jews need Christian blood?" [9] In 1978, fifty years after the incident was hushed up, even after the mass crucifixion of European Jews because of these exact prejudices, some folk in Massena still do not know the answers to those questions. Fortunately such ignorance is more than outweighed by people like Pat McKeon and John Maines of the *Observer,* town historians Eleanor and Marie Elden-Brown, Cole Cummins, the Griffiths and a legion of civilized people who labor to make a reoccurence of the incident impossible.

Still, anti-Semitic ignorance should not come as a surprise. The same morbid curiosity about alleged secret Jewish rites exists all about us. The late George Lincoln Rockwell, the late King Faisal of Saudi Arabia, and Yasir Arafat of the Palestine Liberation Organization all have attested to the veracity of the *Protocols of the Elders of Zion.* Students seeking the papacy's position on the blood libel will find no specific entry on "child-saints" or "ritual murder" in the multi-volume *New Catholic Encyclopedia.* [10] Instead, they may turn to

A Biographical Dictionary of the Saints, compiled by the
Right Reverend F. G. Holweck, domestic prelate to
Pope Piux XI. Here, they will learn: (a) "there is now no
means of ascertaining" whether there was any basis for
the accusation against the Jews in the case of Hugh of
Lincoln; [11] (b) Simon of Trent is said "to have been
cruelly tortured at the age of two" on Maundy Thursday, 1475; [12] (c) in 1287 the Rhenish child-saint Werner
was "martyred by fanatical Jews" who "opened his
veins and bled him to death"; [13] (d) William, the infant
of Norwich, was "murdered by Jews at Paris on Good
Friday";[14] and (e) "there is evidence to support at least
some of the accusations of crimes of superstitious zeal
brought against the Jews throughout Europe during the
latter Middle Ages." [15]

Holweck's work, published contemporaneously with
the events at Massena, must not be dismissed as the
product of a superstitious age. Within the decade, it was
republished with no editorial changes. Moreover, the
contention that Jews, perpetrated ritual murder was giv-
en support recently from a surprising source. In 1971,
Dr. William D. Sharpe, director of laboratories at Columbus Hospital in New York City, published an article
on the subject of ritual murder in the *New York State
Journal of Medicine.* Entitled "The Strange Murder of
William of Norwich, 1144," the article declared that on
the basis of medicolegal analysis the death of a young
boy in the Jewish quarter of Norwich during Easter
Week of 1144 may "possibly be explained by ritual
murder." According to Dr. Sharpe, "Ritual murder can
neither be implicated nor excluded." [16] Reaction to this
statement ranged from astonishment and protest utter-

ed by the Zionist Organization of America, the American Jewish Committee, and the American Jewish Congress, to bemusement on the part of some of Dr. Sharpe's colleague that he had become embroiled in such a controversy. Professional historians especially would question statements of Gentile villagers concerning the Norwich incident, as well as "confessions" wrested from Jews who had been tortured. Dr. Sharpe neither accepted nor discounted those statements; he merely "raises the question."

In a sense, Gentiles ignorant of Jewish rituals are no worse than their Jewish neighbors in Massena, who for the past four decades have sheepishly declined to discuss the matter even with their own children. "Almost no one in the Gentile community knows that any such incident ever happened," wrote Jack Jacobs, "and very few of the Jews here are aware of it, either. Perhaps it is best this way." [17] Others told me, "We have to live here, and to publicize it now would be to plant ideas in the minds of some of the bad elements in town." [18] One uncooperative Jewish storekeeper wanted no part of an historical survey, which could only cause trouble by "encouraging thugs to acts like vandalism" in what he claimed was a happy community. Such sentiments are echoed by one high-ranking official of the American Jewish Congress in New York, who responded to my inquiry for information with the rejoinder: "Why do anything about it now? Why bring it up? *Nobody was killed, were they* [italics mine]?" [19]

To that kind of thinking, one can only respond with the questions phrased by Joseph Stone, J. J. Kauffman, and the others during the weekend of September 22–24,

1928. What if Barbara Griffiths had not been found within twenty-four hours? What if she had been found molested by an animal? By a man? What if she had been found dead, even if the cause of death subsequently was established as accidental? What if the little girl had never been found?

Medieval Europe held no preemption on superstition or perversion. Even in the year 1978, in the most civilized of nations, innocents are wont to slaver at the mouth or confess their sins most grievously at the font of some slack-jawed television soothsayer. Children still wander into the woods (as happened in Youngstown, Ohio, where a four-year-old was recovered after a three-hour search with helicopters), and some fall prey to sadists responsible for the disappearance and/or murder of children whose names (such as Beverly Potts or Sheilah Ann Touhy) are of but momentary importance in the news.

The ignorance and insensitivity of Massena in 1928 were not unique. They could have been duplicated in a hundred other localities in the United States at the time. Although sociologists argue the contrary, they might yet be duplicated in our own day. Given a nation where half those surveyed by the Anti-Defamation League in 1969 indicated a willingness to support an openly anti-Semitic Presidential candidate in times of "acute economic distress," given a nation where Harris and Yankelovich polls report one of every three Americans harboring "hard-core" anti-Semitic attitudes, given a nation where many Gentiles are still reluctant to concede that Jesus was actually a Jew, given a nation where serious thought could be devoted to the construction of

Gerald L. K. Smith's religious shrine in the Ozarks (replete with an Oberammergau-style passion play) or Carl McIntyre's multimillion-dollar replica of Solomon's Temple down in Cape Canaveral, given a nation with a penchant for violence, given a nation that continues to operate with restrictive housing and social club covenants, that freely substitutes the word *Jew* for usury or unethical business dealings, what happened at Massena in 1928 could happen again tomorrow in Berea, Ohio, Hubbard, Ohio, McKees Rocks, Pa., or Saugus, Calif. All that is needed is the right combination: a little town, a lost child, and "different" people. The next time, however, the scapegoats might not be so fortunate. That was the message of the incident at Massena, a warning that was lost amid the personal fears of the Jews in town and the picayune ego conflicts of their national leaders.

NOTES

CHAPTER 1

1. For a discussion of the campaign, see Gustavus Myers, *A History of Bigotry in the United States* (New York: Capricorn edition, 1960), pp. 258–76. Even more spectacular than the reference to making America "100% Catholic, Drunk and Illiterate" (p. 265) is the suggestion (p. 269) that Smith's election would help "contribute a boy to fill a drunkards's grave" and "furnish a daughter to add to the Red Light District by the gin-fizz route."

2. Edmund Moore, *A Catholic Runs for President: The Campaign of 1928* (New York: Ronald, 1956), p. 128.

3. Matthew and Hannah Josephson, *Al Smith: Hero of the Cities* (Boston: Houghton Mifflin, 1969), p. 47.

4. Smith may have been fiercely loyal to his friends, but there is nothing in the record or the reminiscences of his key aide Judge Joseph Proskauer, *A Segment of My Times* (New York: Farrar, Straus, 1950), to connote servility to Tammany politicians.

5. Josephson, *Al Smith,* pp. 361–62.

6. Among the better works on the Klan are David Chambers, *Hooded Americanism; The First Century of the Ku Klux Klan, 1865–1965* (Garden City, N. Y.: Doubleday, 1965); Henry Fry, *The Modern Ku Klux Klan* (New York: Negro Universities Press, 1960);

Notes

Kenneth Jackson, *The Ku Klux Klan in the City, 1915–1930* (New York: Oxford University Press, 1957); William Randel, *The Ku Klux Klan: A Century of Infamy* (Philadelphia: Chilton, 1965); and Arnold Rice, *The Ku Klux Klan in American Politics* (Washington: Public Affairs Press, 1962).

7. Indicative of the hysteria sweeping the nation that year: when someone reported the pope was about to arrive at North Manchester, Ind. on a northbound train one afternoon in September 1928, 1,500 persons turned out to the depot to watch. See Moore, *A Catholic Runs for President,* p. 148.

8. Hoover's failure to react swiftly to the circular letter of Virginia committeewoman Willie Caldwell (in which she advised voters to "save us from being romanzied and rum-ridden") earned him several editorial censures from the *New York Times,* September 25, p. 30, and September 26, p. 1.

9. This unfortunate "test" was codrafted by Father Francis Duffy, a World War I hero. It appeared as "Catholic and Patriot: Reply to C. C. Marshall," *Atlantic,* 139 (1927): 721–728.

10. Richard O'Connor, *The First Hurrah: A Biography of Alfred E. Smith* (New York: Putnam, 1970), p. 212.

11. Josephson, *Al Smith,* pp. 380–81.

12. *Progressive Democracy: Addresses and State Papers of Alfred E. Smith* (New York: Harcourt, Brace, 1928), pp. 253–254.

13. Notes made by Alfred Smith for campaign speech, Oklahoma City, Sept. 20, 1928, in Alfred E. Smith Papers, Museum of the City of New York.

14. Josephson, *Al Smith,* pp. 383–384.

15. *New York Times,* Sept. 21, 1928, pp. 1–2.

16. Moore, *A Catholic Runs for President,* pp. 136–140.

CHAPTER 2

1. I am actually being more gentle than others who have traversed the North Country. Carl Carmer writes: "The country north of Malone flattens toward the plain that borders the St. Lawrence River. Most of it is far from fertile, as the little, desolate shacks of farmers attest. It is rocky, scrub-filled, monotonous. It is a country of heartbreaking poverty, of ignorance and incredible shiftlessness, but it is also a land of ironic humor." *Listen for a Lonesome Drum: A New York State Chronicle* (New York: Blue Ribbon, 1936), p. 298.

Notes

2. *New York: A Guide to the Empire State,* WPA Writers Program (New York: Oxford University Press, 1940), pp. 27-36.

3. Leonard Prince, Nick Podgurski, and Richard Peer (eds.), *The Massena Story,* special publication of Chamber of Commerce, 1958, p. 2.

4. *New York: A Guide to the Empire State,* p. 531.

5. Flyer, titled "Massena, New York," compiled by Massena Chamber of Commerce, Mar. 19, 1971, p. 1.

6. "André Masséna," *Encyclopaedia Britannica,* vol. 14, p. 1034.

7. *The Massena Story,* pp. 6-8.

8. *Ibid.,* p. 9.

9. *Ibid.,* pp. 10-11.

10. Undated release of Massena Chamber of Commerce, pp. 4-5.

11. *The Massena Story,* pp. 32-43. See also a flyer of the Chamber of Commerce titled "St. Lawrence Seaway Power Developments."

12. Interview with town historian Marie Elden-Brown, Massena, Aug. 20, 1971.

13. By 1940 it was estimated that perhaps as many as 60 percent of the people living and working in the Malone, Plattsburgh, and Cohoes regions belonged to the French-Canadian ethnic group. *New York: A Guide to the Empire State,* p. 109.

14. Rudolf Glanz, "Source Materials on the History of Jewish Immigration to the United States, 1800-1880," *YIVO Annual of Jewish Social Sciences* (1951) vol. 6, pp. 128-29. Glanz notes that Polish Jews had begun to settle in Ottawa as early as 1863 (p. 115) and quotes Theodor Griesinger of Stuttgart to the effect that "eleven times out of ten the peddler is a Jew" (p. 133).

15. *New York: A Guide to the Empire State,* p. 530.

16. Carmer, *Listen for a Lonesome Drum,* p. 195.

17. Interview with Marie Elden-Brown.

18. *The American Jewish Yearbook, 1928-1929,* p. 227, places the number of Jews in Massena at 102.

19. Interview with Dora Shulkin Cohen, Massena, Aug. 20, 1971.

20. Interview with Marie Elden-Brown.

21. Interviews with Seward Hanmer, Massena, Aug. 23, 1971; Ella Lahey, Aug. 22, 1971; Jack Jacobs, Aug. 20, 1971; and Eli Friedman, Syracuse, Aug. 27, 1971.

22. Interview with Cole Cummins, Massena, Aug. 22, 1971.

23. Interview with Ben Shulkin, Rome, N. Y., Aug. 25, 1971.

24. Interview with Busse Dumas, Massena, Aug. 22, 1971.

25. *Massena Observer,* Sept. 10, 1928, p. 1.

CHAPTER 3

1. *Massena Observer,* Sept. 20, 1928, pp. 1–2.

2. Background information on the Griffiths family comes from interviews with Dave and Marion Griffiths, Aug. 21–22, 1971, and Dec. 20 and 27, 1977, and from the Griffiths File, Massena Town Historical Society, Massena, N. Y.

3. According to Byron Dalrymple, better than 90 percent of the kills of black bear take place in the Adirondacks and Catskills, for these animals "rarely venture out of the mountains." *Complete Guide to Hunting Across North America* (New York and London: Harper and Row, 1970), p. 87.

4. Interview with Marie Elden-Brown, Aug. 20, 1971.

5. Interview with Cole Cummins, Aug. 22, 1971. The body had badly decomposed and was little better than a skeleton by the time a group of children chanced upon it.

6. George Ure was one of the few uncommunicative old-timers from Massena. When contacted in August 1971, he refused to discuss the incident. He passed away several years ago.

7. *The Massena Story,* pp. 22–23.

8. Roy Countryman should not be confused with Roy Contryman. The latter did work at Alcoa for a while before becoming a professional nurse. He and his wife were decent people and close friends of the Griffithses. See p. 45.

9. Interview with Cole Cummins, Aug. 22, 1971. People who defend the firemen always point out that a Jew, Joseph Stone, was appointed treasurer of the volunteer fire organization.

10. Interview with *Massena Observer* editor Leonard Prince, Aug. 20, 1971.

11. Interviews with Jack Jacobs, Aug. 20, 1971; Dora Cohen, Aug. 20, 1971; and Cole Cummins, Aug. 22, 1971.

12. Interview with Chamber of Commerce secretary Ernest Wagar, Aug. 20, 1971.

13. Interview with Marie Elden-Brown, Aug. 20, 1971.

14. Massena Chief of Police Dale Wright accompanied me through the ancient vault that houses township records in City Hall, Aug. 23, 1971. Perhaps it was just coincidence, perhaps sloppy record-keeping, but there was no blotter for the crucial fall months of

1928. Chief Wright, a young man with no background on the incident, was somewhat appalled by San Jule's records.

15. San Jule File, Massena Town Historical Society.

16. Interview with former State Highway Patrol Captain Harry Hollander, Massena, Aug. 22, 1971.

17. Carl Carmer, *Listen for a Lonesome Drum,* pp. 294, 304.

18. *Ibid.,* p. 304.

19. Interview with former State Highway Patrolman Joe Burke, Malone, N. Y., Aug. 22, 1971.

20. Interview with Jack Jacobs, Aug. 21, 1971. It was a view supported by Amadeo Cappione, an Italian immigrant who worked for Utica Club Beer at the time. Recalling Mickey McCann, Cappione said, "He was a rough trooper. But then, anyone with a uniform was rough at that time." Interview, Jan. 2, 1978.

21. Interview with Joe Burke, Aug. 22, 1971.

22. *Massena Observer,* Sept. 20, 1928, p. 4.

23. For the remainder of information concerning events about the Griffiths homestead that Saturday evening, Sept. 22, 1928, I am primarily indebted to interviews with Mr. and Mrs. Griffiths, noted above.

24. *Massena Observer,* Sept. 27, 1928, p. 1.

CHAPTER 4

1. Background information on the Shulkin family was obtained mainly from interviews with Ben Shulkin, Rome, N. Y., Aug. 25, 1971; Dora Shulkin Cohen, Massena, Aug. 20, 1971, and Miami, Fla., Dec. 28, 1977; Mimi Shulkin Klein, Miami, Dec. 28, 1977; and their cousin Lou Greenblatt, Miami, Dec. 28, 1977. Mr. Greenblatt has been doing a history of Jews in Saint Lawrence County and interviewed Jake Shulkin prior to his death in 1964. Unfortunately, Mr. Shulkin's account of what transpired in Massena in 1928 does not jibe with contemporary records in many details.

2. Interview with Minnie Slavin, Massena, Aug. 21, 1971.

3. Interview with Dora Shulkin Cohen, Dec. 28, 1977.

4. Interview with Marie Elden-Brown, Massena, Aug. 20, 1971. A friend of Jake Shulkin's, Saul Rosenbaum was just as laudatory. "He was a smart man," Rosenbaum noted in an interview in August 1971. "He knew everything from A to Z."

Notes

5. According to her son Ben, "She could get things on the table in no time." Interview, Aug. 25, 1971.

6. Interview with Minnie Slavin, Aug. 21, 1971.

7. Interview with Ben Shulkin, Aug. 25, 1971.

8. According to Dora Cohen, "My father wasn't going to vote for Al Smith. Nobody voted Democrat then. Up to that time, everyone in Massena voted Republican, even the Jews. That was before Roosevelt, the great friend of the Jews, who was no friend." Interview, Dec. 28, 1977.

9. *American Jewish Yearbook, 1929,* vol. 31 (Philadelphia: Jewish Publication Society of America), pp. 21–98.

10. *New York Times,* Sept. 15, 1928, p. 8, and Sept. 20, 1928, p. 9.

11. Interview with Dora Cohen, Dec. 18, 1977.

12. Interview with Mimi Klein, Dec. 28, 1977.

13. It was an impression reinforced when Sarah Shulkin spent the last several years of her life in a nursing home in Syracuse before her death in the fall of 1977.

14. Interview with Ben Shulkin, Aug. 25, 1971.

15. *Ibid.* For contemporary insight into hypomania, see Francis Dercum, *A Clinical Manual of Mental Diseases* (Philadelphia and London: W. B. Saunders, 1918), pp. 94–98; and Arthur Noyes, *Modern Clinical Psychiatry* (Philadelphia and London: W. B. Saunders, 1935), pp. 137–139. Subjects are usually of pyknic (rounded, fatty) physique, with cyclothymic temperaments. The age of onset of the disorder, twice as common among men as women, is between fifteen and twenty-five. Individuals may be given to extravagant gestures, boastful declamations, and broken speech uttered with abnormal rapidity. They are given to hallucinations, crude jokes, tears, and verbal abuse. All of the above seem to fit Willie and his brother Harold.

16. Interview with Dora Cohen and Mimi Klein, Dec. 28, 1977.

17. Interview with Jack Jacobs, Aug. 21, 1977. Jacobs believed Shulkin to be "schizophrenic" but "harmless."

18. Interview with Mimi Klein, Dec. 28, 1977.

19. Interview with Leonard Prince, editor, *Massena Observer,* Aug. 20, 1971.

20. Interview with Ernest Wagar, secretary, Massena Chamber of Commerce, Aug. 20, 1971. Wagar referred to a later incident, when Willie threatened police with an ax when they came to appropriate his driver's license.

21. Interview with Harry Levine, Massena, Aug. 20, 1971.

22. Interview with Ben Shulkin, Aug. 25, 1971.
23. Interview with Dora Cohen, Aug. 20, 1971. Equally protective but probably just as inaccurate in her reading of Willie was Minnie Slavin, who said he was "a sweet boy who was just retarded." Interview, Aug. 21, 1971.
24. Interview with Ben Shulkin, Aug. 25, 1971.
25. Arthur Noyes and Edith Haydon, *Textbook of Psychiatric Nursing* (New York: MacMillan, 1951), p. 310.
26. *Ibid.,* pp. 330–333, 309–310.
27. Noyes, *Modern Clinical Psychiatry,* p. 156.
28. "Insanity," in R. J. Zwi Werblowsky and Geoffrey Wigoder (eds.), *The Encyclopedia of the Jewish Religion* (New York: Holt, Rinehart and Winston, 1965), pp. 201–202.

CHAPTER 5

1. Lee M. Friedman, *Pilgrims in a New Land* (Philadelphia: Jewish Publication Society of America, 1948), pp. 110–111.
2. *Ibid.*
3. Interview with Ben Shulkin, Rome, N. Y., Aug. 23, 1971.
4. Interviews with Eli Friedman, Miami, Fla., and Jack Jacobs, Massena, Jan. 2, 1978. The town had no Jewish doctor until 1935.
5. Information on Albert Comnas was obtained from interviews with Dora Cohen, Aug. 20, 1971; Jack Jacobs, Aug. 20–21, 1971; Eli Friedman, Aug. 24, 1971; and Cole Cummins, Aug. 22, 1971.
6. Interviews with Anna Pilialoglous, Aug. 22, 1971; and Abe Kauffman, Aug. 20, 1971.
7. Interview with Saul Rosenbaum, Aug. 21, 1971.
8. *Ibid.*
9. See "Salonika," *Universal Jewish Encyclopedia,* vol. 9 (1943), pp. 327–329; and "Greece," *Encyclopedia Judaica,* vol. 7 (1971), pp. 875–878.
10. Malcolm Hay, *Europe and the Jews* (Boston: Beacon, 1950), p. 28.
11. Werner Keller, *Diaspora: The Post-Biblical History of the Jews* (New York: Harcourt, Brace and World, 1966), p. 101.
12. Hay, *Europe and the Jews,* p. 29.
13. Jacob Marcus, *The Jew in the Medieval World* (Philadelphia: Jewish Publication Society of America, 1960), pp. 44–46; and Leon Poliakov, *A History of Anti-Semitism,* vol. 1 (New York: Schocken,

Notes

1965), pp. 107–108. On early church history, see James Parkes, *The Conflict of the Church and the Synagogue* (New York: Atheneum, 1969).

14. Joshua Trachtenberg, *The Devil and the Jews* (Philadelphia: Jewish Publication Society of America, 1948), pp. 109–124)

15. On the *foetor Judaicus* and Jewish need for blood, see Trachtenberg, *op. cit.,* pp. 47–52. *The Devil & The Jews*

16. Joshua Trachtenberg, *Jewish Magic and Superstition* (New York: Atheneum, 1970) pp. 7–10, and *The Devil and the Jews,* pp. 50–52.

17. For the Polna affair, see Simon Dubnow, *History of the Jews from the Congress of Vienna to the Emergence of Hitler,* vol. 5, trans. Moshe Spiegel (New York: Yoseloff, 1973), pp. 495–496.

18. Hay, *Europe and the Jews,* p. 128.

19. *Ibid.,* p. 123.

20. Edward Flannery, *The Anguish of the Jews* (New York: Macmillan, 1964), pp. 98–101.

21. Edward Synan, *The Popes and the Jews in the Middle Ages* (New York: Macmillan, 1965), pp. 103–124; and Poliakov, *History of Anti-Semitism,* pp. 59–63.

22. "Blood Accusation," Jewish Encyclopedia, vol. 3 (1902), pp. 260–267; and "Blood Accusation," *Universal Jewish Encyclopedia,* vol. 2, (1940), pp. 407–410.

23. On the Beiliss affair, see Alexander Tager, *The Decay of Czarism: The Beiliss Trial* (Philadelphia: Jewish Publication Society of America, 1935); Arnold Margolin, *The Jews of Eastern Europe* (New York: Thomas Seltzer, 1926); Maurice Samuel, *Blood Accusation: The Strange History of the Beiliss Case* (New York: Knopf, 1956); and Bernard Malamud, *The Fixer* (New York: Farrar, Straus and Giroux, 1966).

24. Interviews with Eli Friedman, Aug. 23, 1971, and Jan. 2, 1978.

25. Interview with Lou Greenblatt, Dec. 29, 1977.

26. Interview with Jack Jacobs, Aug. 21, 1971. Jacobs contributed a chapter to the bicentennial publication on Massena, in which he referred to the "brief but ugly incident." Here, he quoted the Greek as saying, "In the Old Country, people would suspect the Jews of foul play." *A History of Massena, The Orphan Town* (Bicentennial Commission, Eleanor Dumas, chairman, 1977;), pp. 140ff.

27. Interview with Saul Rosenbaum, Aug. 21, 1971.

28. Interview with Dora Cohen, Dec. 28, 1977.

29. Interview with Mimi Klein, Dec. 29, 1977.

30. Interview with Dora Cohen, Dec. 28, 1977. Cole Cummins

said practically the same thing: "He was around, just strolling around. He used to come downtown to have lunch or a soft drink. They stepped out to question him and worked on what Willie said. He was abnormal." Interview, Jan. 2, 1978.

31. Interviews with Mimi Klein and Lou Greenblatt, Dec. 29, 1977.
32. Interview with Jack Jacobs, Aug. 21, 1971.
33. Interview with Ben Shulkin, Aug. 23, 1971.
34. Interview with Jack Jacobs, Aug. 21, 1971.
35. Interview with Mimi Klein, Dec. 29, 1977.
36. Interview with Harry Levine, Aug. 20, 1971.
37. *New York Post,* Oct. 4, 1928, p. 5.

CHAPTER 6

1. Leonard Prince, Nick Podgurski, and Richard Peer (eds.), *The Massena Story,* special publication of Chamber of Commerce, 1958, p. 12.
2. Interview with Eli Friedman, Aug. 24, 1971.
3. Hawes File, Massena Town Historical Society.
4. Interview with Cole Cummins, Aug. 22, 1971.
5. The *Massena Observer* in March 1930 carried a listing of Hawes's purported accomplishments.
6. Interview with Ella Lahey, Aug. 22, 1971.
7. Interview with Ernest Wagar, Aug. 20, 1971.
8. Interview with Seward Hanmer, Aug. 23, 1971.
9. Interviews with Seward Hanmer, Aug. 23, 1971; and Leonard Prince, Aug. 20, 1971.
10. Interview with Dora Cohen, Aug. 20, 1971.
11. Interview with Jack Jacobs, Aug. 20, 1971.
12. Interview with Seward Hanmer, Aug. 23, 1971.
13. Interview with Leonard Prince, Aug. 20, 1971.
14. Interview with Saul Rosenbaum, Aug. 20, 1971.
15. *Ibid.,* and interview, Jan. 2, 1978.
16. Interview with Cole Cummins, Aug. 22, 1971.
17. Interview with Busse Dumas, Jan. 2, 1978.
18. Major newspapers repeatedly misidentified Willie as "Joseph Shulkin" or "Jacob Shaulkin." For Lieutenant Heim's report, see "Massena Blood Libel Scotched," *American Hebrew,* Oct. 12, 1928, pp. 751-752.
19. Letter from Hawes to Boris Smolar, *Jewish Daily Bulletin,* Oct.

3, 1928, vol. 5, p. 4. Massena File, American Jewish Committee Library, New York City.

20. Interviews with Dora Cohen and Mimi Klein, Dec. 29, 1977.

21. *New York Post,* Oct. 4, 1928, p. 5.

22. Letter of Hawes to Smolar.

23. Report of Lieutenant Heim, in *American Hebrew.*

24. Undated clippings in Massena File, New York State Police, Albany Campus. According to Superintendent William E. Kirwan, "all of the official records in the case were purged in the period of 1943–44 and the only existing records are newspaper clips." Letter to author, Aug. 25, 1971.

25. Report of Lieutenant Heim in *American Hebrew.*

26. Letter of Hawes to Smolar.

27. Letter of Joseph Stone to American Jewish Committee, Sept. 28, 1928, in American Jewish Committee Library, Massena File.

CHAPTER 7

1. Interviews with Dora Cohen and Mimi Klein, Dec. 29, 1977.

2. Interview with Ben Shulkin, Aug. 25, 1971.

3. Interviews with Jack Jacobs, Aug. 21, 1971; Saul Rosenbaum, Aug. 20, 1971; and Eli Friedman, Aug. 24, 1971. Joe Stone supposedly suffered from poor health most of his life, and died of kidney failure in 1933 at the age of forty-six.

4. Abe Kauffman declares, "This is as close as you can get it. The way you describe it is exactly my idea, as accurate as you can get it." Interview, Jan. 3, 1978.

5. Interview with Kauffman, Aug. 20, 1971.

6. On the Kishinev pogrom, see "Kishinev," *Universal Jewish Encyclopedia,* vol. 6, (1942), pp. 403–404; "Kishinev," *Encyclopedia Judaica,* vol. 10 (1971), pp. 1063–1070; Cyrus Adler, *The Voice of America on Kishinev,* (Philadelphia: Jewish Publication Society of America, 1904); Max Margolis and Alexander Marx, *A History of the Jewish People* (Philadelphia: Jewish Publication Society of America, 1927), pp. 709–711, 714–715; and Ismar Elbogen, *A Century of Jewish Life* (Philadelphia: Jewish Publication Society of America, 1944), pp. 376–389.

7. On Leo Frank, see "Frank, Leo, Case of" *Universal Jewish Encyclopedia,* vol. 4 (1941), pp. 394–395; "Frank, Leo Max," *Encyclopedia Judaica,* vol. 7 (1971), pp. 73–74; Gustavus Myers, *His-*

tory of Bigotry in the United States, pp. 202–210; and Harry Golden, *A Little Girl Is Dead* (Cleveland: World, 1965).

8. *Allgemeine Zeitung des Judentums* (1850), p. 593, cited in Rudolf Glanz, "Source Materials on the History of Jewish Immigration to the United States, 1800–1880," *YIVO Annual, Jewish Social Sciences,* vol. 6 (1951), p. 147.

9. Morris Schappes, *Documentary History of Jews in the United States* (New York: Citadel, 1950), p. 19.

10. Interview with Abe Kauffman, Jan. 3, 1978.

11. Letter of Jake Shulkin to Rabbi Wise, Sept. 25, 1928, Massena Folder, Wise Papers, American Jewish Historical Society, Brandeis University, Waltham, Mass.

12. "American Jewish Committee," *Universal Jewish Encyclopedia,* vol. 1 (1939), pp. 242–247; and Naomi Cohen, *Not Free to Desist: The American Jewish Committee, 1906–66* (Philadelphia: Jewish Publication Society of America, 1972).

13. Moses Leavitt, *The JDC Story, 1914–1952* (New York: Joint Distribution Committee, 1953).

14. Nathan Caro Belth, "Louis Marshall," *Universal Jewish Encyclopedia,* vol. 7 (1942), pp. 380–385.

15. Gustavus Myers, *History of Bigotry in the United States,* pp. 277–301.

16. Norman Cohn, *Warrant for Genocide: The Myth of the Jewish World-Conspiracy and the Protocols of the Elders of Zion,* (New York: Harper, 1966), pp. 73–76.

17. *Ibid.,* pp. 60–65, 269–289.

18. On the Sapira affair, see the *New York Times,* Apr. 1, 1927, p. 4; Apr. 2, 1927, p. 4; Apr. 5, 1927, p. 29; Apr. 6, 1927, p. 29; Apr. 7, 1927, p. 22; Apr. 8, 1927, p. 6; Apr. 10, 1927, p. 19; and Myers, *History of Bigotry,* pp. 300–302.

19. *New York Times,* July 8, 1927, p. 1.

20. *New York Times,* July 9, 1927, p. 12.

21. At the time, there was a rumor that Sapira had been bought off personally by a gift from Ford of $140,000. *New York Times,* July 26, 1927, p. 22. On Ford's retraction, see Myers, *History of Bigotry,* pp. 301–313; and Cohn, *Warrant for Genocide,* pp. 158–164.

22. Other Ford publications included *The World's Foremost Problem* (1920), *Jewish Activities in the United States* (1921), *Jewish Influences in American Life* (1921), *and Aspects of Jewish Power in the United States* (1922).

23. Charles Stember et al., *Jews in the Mind of America* (New York: Basic Books, 1966), pp. 138–39.

Notes

24. Trachtenberg, *The Devil and the Jews,* p. 227.
25. Joseph Gaer, *The Legend of the Wandering Jew* (New York: Mentor, 1961).
26. "American Jewish Committee," p. 242.
27. "Jewish Telegraph Agency," *Universal Jewish Encyclopedia,* vol. 6 (1942), pp. 142–143.
28. Interview with Boris Smolar, New York City, Aug. 25, 1971.
29. "It Happened Before Kol Nidre: Smolar's Recollections of Massena Blood Libel," *Detroit Jewish News,* Oct. 11, 1965, p. 2.
30. *Ibid.*
31. *Ibid.* Smolar prides himself on accuracy, but there is reason to believe his account is riddled with error, much as Lee Friedman's. Samuel Brennglass assured me (Sept. 18, 1971) that there was no Sunday train into Massena in 1928. Smolar identifies the rabbi as "Bert Brennglass" and also claims "the chief of police" was responsible for the incident and that he (Smolar) interviewed the chief at headquarters. Mayor Hawes concedes that he was interviewed by Smolar several days after Barbara Griffiths was found. An undated memo from Bernard Richards to Wise in the Wise Papers at Brandeis also notes that the JTA "had a man on the spot and he is back with a report." So, too, a letter from Jake Shulkin to Stephen Wise in the Massena Folder of the Wise Papers mentions "a representative of the Jewish Telegraph Agency" who was "here Friday and Saturday morning" (almost a week after the incident). Whatever the case, Abe Kauffman summed up most people's attitudes about Smolar when he says, "He came up here, nosing around."

CHAPTER 8

1. Interview with Cole Cummins, Jan. 2, 1978.
2. *Ibid.*
3. Interview with Saul Rosenbaum, Aug. 20, 1971.
4. "Massena Blood Libel Scotched," *American Hebrew,* Oct. 12, 1928, p. 151.
5. "It Happened Before Kol Nidre," *Detroit Jewish News,* Oct. 1, 1965, p. 2.
6. Interviews with Abe Kauffman, Aug. 20, 1971; and Jack Jacobs, Aug. 21, 1971, and Jan. 2, 1978. Jacobs admitted recently that he does not recall everything that happened at the time. "I may be projecting what I think I ought to know or what I recall hearing afterward," he told me.

7. Letter of Jake Shulkin to Rabbi Wise, Sept. 25, 1928, Wise Papers, Massena File, American Jewish Historical Society, Brandeis.
8. Interview with Jeannette Rosenbaum, Aug. 21, 1971.
9. Interview with Minnie Slavin, Aug. 21, 1971.
10. Interview with Abe Kauffman, Aug. 20, 1971.
11. Letter of Shulkin to Wise.
12. *Ibid.*
13. Harry Levine said (Aug. 20, 1971), "One man wanted to be a big shot and gave out stupid statements." Jack Jacobs on the incident (Aug. 21, 1971): "You ask a deranged boy and one who knows not one shred of Jewish knowledge." Mimi Klein (Dec. 28, 1977): "Morris Goldberg did the Jews a disservice. He, at least, was stable."
14. Letter of Shulkin to Wise.
15. *Ibid.*
16. Letter of Mickey McCann to Rabbi Brennglass, Oct. 4, 1928, in Wise Papers, Massena File, American Jewish Historical Society, Brandeis.
17. Interviews with Samuel Brennglass, Sept. 18, 1971; Dora Cohen, Aug. 20, 1971; Jack Jacobs, Aug. 20, 1971; and Eli Friedman, Aug. 24, 1971.
18. J. H. Hertz (ed.), *Pentateuch and Haftorahs,* (London: Soncino, 1962), p. 487.
19. "Shehitah," *Jewish Encyclopedia,* vol. 2 (Funk & Wagnalls, 1905), pp. 253-257; and "Slaughtering, Ritual," *Universal Jewish Encyclopedia,* vol. 9 (1943), pp. 562-565.
20. The practice was strongly opposed as "pagan" by Nahmanides, Joseph Caro, and other leading Jewish figures in the early modern period. See "Kapparah," *Jewish Encyclopedia,* vol. 7 (Funk & Wagnalls, 1904), pp. 435-436. For the continued application, I am indebted to my friend and mentor, Joseph Podgorsky Hill of Youngstown, Ohio.
21. Lee Friedman, *Pilgrims in a New Land,* p. 111.
22. "It Happened Before Kol Nidre," p. 2.
23. "Massena Blood Libel Scotched," p. 151.
24. Letter of Shulkin to Wise.
25. Interview with Eli Friedman, Jan. 2, 1978.
26. Harry Schneiderman, "Review of the Year 5689," in *American Jewish Yearbook,* vol. 31 (Jewish Publication Society of America, 1929), p. 21.
27. *New York Times,* Oct. 3, 1928, p. 34.
28. Friedman, *Pilgrims in a New Land,* p. 112.
29. Letter of Shulkin to Wise.

30. Interview with Jack Jacobs, Aug. 21, 1971.
31. Interview with Lou Greenblatt, Dec. 29, 1977.
32. Reconstructed from interviews with Ben Shulkin, Dora Cohen, Eli Friedman, Jack Jacobs, Abe Kauffman, and Lou Greenblatt.
33. Interview with Cole Cummins, Jan. 2, 1978.

CHAPTER 9

1. Interview with Eli Friedman, Syracuse, N.Y., Aug. 23, 1971.
2. Letter of Jake Shulkin to Stephen Wise, Sept. 25, 1928, Massena File, Wise Papers, American Jewish Archives, Brandeis University; letter of Shulkin to Louis Marshall, Sept. 23, 1928, and letter of Julius Frank to Marshall, Sept. 26, 1928, Massena File, Library of American Jewish Committee, New York City.
3. Interview with Eli Friedman, Miami, Fla., Jan. 2, 1978.
4. "It Happened Before Kol Nidre: Smolar's Recollections of Massena Blood Libel Case," *Detroit Jewish News,* Oct. 1, 1965, p. 2.
5. Interview with Dave Griffiths, Aug. 22, 1971.
6. *Ibid.*
7. *Massena Observer,* Sept. 27, 1928, p. 1. The Thursday edition bannered "Four Year Old Child Lost in Woods Twenty Four Hours," then added the subhead "Little Barbara, Daughter of Mr. and Mrs. David Griffith [sic], Out All Last Saturday Nite Alone, Found Sunday Afternoon." There was no mention of the ritual-murder charge in the lengthy article. An additional irony was the appearance of a large Shulkin and Slavin's advertisement on p. 2 of this edition.
8. Interview with Marion Griffiths, Aug. 21, 1971.
9. *Massena Observer,* Sept. 27, 1928, p. 1.
10. Interview with Dave Griffiths, Dec. 21, 1977.
11. *Massena Observer,* Sept. 27, 1928, p. 1.
12. Interview with Cole Cummins, Aug. 22, 1971.
13. Interview with Cissy Dumas, Jan. 2, 1978.
14. *Massena Observer,* Sept. 27, 1928, p. 1.
15. *Ibid.*

CHAPTER 10

1. "It Happened Before Kol Nidre: Smolar's Recollections of Massena Blood Libel Case," *Detroit Jewish News,* Oct. 1, 1965, p. 1.

2. Interviews with Jack Jacobs, Aug. 20, 1971; Abe Kauffman, Aug. 20, 1971; Saul Rosenbaum, Aug. 22, 1971; and Eli Friedman, Aug. 23, 1971.

3. Letter of Jake Shulkin to Rabbi Wise, Sept. 25, 1928, Massena Folder, Wise Papers, American Jewish Archives, Brandeis University.

4. On the significance of Yom Kippur, see notes on Leviticus 16:34, in J. H. Hertz (ed.), *Pentateuch and Haftorahs* (London: Soncino, 1962), p. 485.

5. Morris Silverman (ed.), *High Holiday Prayer Book* (Bridgeport, Conn.: United Synagogue of America by Prayer Book Press, 1951), p. 207.

6. Cecil Roth, *The Spanish Inquisition* (New York: Norton, 1964).

7. On Numbers 15:26, see Hertz, *Pentateuch and Haftorahs,* p. 632.

8. *High Holiday Prayer Book,* pp. 227–246.

9. Interview with Jack Jacobs, Jan. 2, 1978.

10. Interview with Louis Greenblatt, Dec. 29, 1977.

11. Interviews with Dora Cohen, Mimi Klein, and Louis Greenblatt, Dec. 29, 1977.

12. Interview with Ben Shulkin, Aug. 25, 1971.

13. The rabbi's talk has been pieced together from reminiscences of Ben Shulkin, Jack Jacobs, Eli Friedman, Abe Kauffman, and Saul Rosenbaum.

CHAPTER 11

1. That Stone called Heim is attested by clippings, Massena File, New York State Police, State Campus, Albany, N. Y.

2. For this promenade and its contents, I am indebted to Eli Friedman and Saul Rosenbaum, interviews, Aug. 23 and 21, 1971.

3. Tacitus, 5:2ff, in *The Histories,* trans. Alfred Church and William Brodribb (New York: Random House, Modern Library, 1942), pp. 657–660.

4. Joshua Trachtenberg, *The Devil and the Jews* (Philadelphia: Jewish Publication Society of America, 1948), pp. 88–97.

5. On the "Image of the Jews," see Poliakov, *A History of Anti-Semitism,* pp. 123–164; James Parkes, *The Conflict of the Church and the Synagogue,* pp. 94–117; Edward Synan, *The Popes and the Jews in the Middle Ages,* pp. 31–50; and Edward Flannery, *The Anguish of the Jews,* pp. 25–63.

Notes

6. "Blood Accusation," *Jewish Encyclopedia,* vol. 3 (Funk & Wagnalls, 1902), pp. 260–267.
7. Malcolm Hay, *Europe and the Jews* (Boston: Beacon, 1950), pp. 140–160.
8. Interview with Eli Friedman, Aug. 23, 1971.
9. Some dispute exists over where the actual meeting took place. Freidman says it was upstairs, in the boys' department at Stone's store. Heim's official report of Sept. 26, 1928, says the synagogue. See Report of Lieutenant Heim, American Jewish Committee Archives, General Correspondence File, 1906–1932, Massena Folder.
10. Interview with Seward Hanmer, Aug. 22, 1971.
11. *Ibid.*
12. *Ibid.*
13. Report of Lieutenant Heim.
14. Interview with Abe Kauffman, Aug. 20, 1971.
15. Letter of Joe Stone to American Jewish Committee, Sept. 28, 1928, American Jewish Committee Archives, New York.
16. Statement of Mayor Hawes to Smolar, *Jewish Daily Bulletin,* vol. 5, Oct. 3, 1928, p. 4.
17. Letter of Hawes to Wise, *New York Post,* Oct. 4, 1928. p. 5.

CHAPTER 12

1. Interview with Abe Kauffman, Jan. 3, 1978.
2. Letter of Hawes to Wise, Oct. 2, 1928, Wise Papers, Massena Folder, American Jewish Historical Society, Brandeis University.
3. Interview with Ernest Wagar, Aug. 20, 1971.
4. Interviews with Dora Cohen and Jack Jacobs, Aug. 20, 1971.
5. Interview with Seward Hanmer, Aug. 22, 1971.
6. Interviews with Abe Kauffman and Jack Jacobs, Aug. 20, 1971.
7. Interview with Saul Rosenbaum, Aug. 21, 1971.
8. "It Happened Before Kol Nidre," *Detroit Jewish News,* Oct. 1, 1965, p. 2.
9. *New York Post,* Oct. 2, 1928, p. 1.
10. Letter of Marshall to Warner, Oct. 11, 1928, American Jewish Committee Archives, General Correspondence File, 1906–1932, Massena Folder.
11. *Ibid.*
12. *New York Times,* Oct. 3, 1928, p. 34.
13. *Ibid.*

14. *Ibid.*
15. "Wise, Stephen Samuel," *Universal Jewish Encyclopedia,* vol. 10 (1943), p. 543.
16. "American Jewish Congress," *Universal Jewish Encyclopedia,* vol. 1 (1939), pp. 247–52; and *To the Jews of America: The Jewish Congress Versus the American Jewish Committee* (New York: Jewish Congress Organizing Committee, 1915), pp. 5–8.
17. For a view of how "Young Turks" become "old Establishment," see Saul Friedman, *No Haven for the Oppressed* (Detroit: Wayne State University Press, 1973), pp. 129–154. Rabbi Wise's performance in World War II leaves much to be desired.
18. Telegram, Bernard Richards to Shulkin, Sept. 29, 1928, Wise Papers, American Jewish Historical Society, New York.
19. Letter, Wise to Shulkin, Sept. 29, 1928, Wise Papers, American Jewish Historical Society, New York. Wrote Wise: "I do not propose to let this matter rest until there be the fullest explanation on the part of those responsible for the rumour, to the end that the apology may be made to the Jewish community which, in a sense, represents American Israel and has the honor of American Israel in its keeping."
20. Letter, Wise to Ellis, Sept. 29, 1928, Wise Papers.
21. Letter, Wise to Major Warner, Sept. 29, 1928, Wise Papers.
22. Letter, Wise to Hawes, Sept. 29, 1928, Wise Papers.
23. Memorandum, Wise to Richards, Sept. 28, 1928, Wise Papers.
24. Letter, Governor Smith to Wise, Oct. 3, 1928, Wise Papers.
25. Message read and recorded at American Jewish Congress, Oct. 3, 1928. See also Massena Memorandum, Oct. 9, 1928, Wise Papers.
26. Morton Rosenstock, *Louis Marshall: Defender of Jewish Rights* (Detroit: Wayne State University Press, 1965), p. 266.
27. Edmund Moore, *A Catholic Runs for President: The Campaign of 1928* (New York: Ronald, 1956), pp. 114–115.
28. See correspondence with M. W. Jacoby, Brooklyn, Joseph Lazarowitz, Columbus, M. S. Kemp, Mountain View, Julian Mayer, New York City, and Edward Bennett, Little Rock, in Smith Papers, Library, New York State Education Department, Albany, N. Y. The one intriguing missive that has survived came from a member of the U.S. Senate Committee on Naval Affairs. Unsigned and undated, it reminded Smith of the struggle waged by Daniel O'Connell on behalf of religious liberty in England in the previous century. The note concluded: "O'Connell flatly stated that the Catholics would not accept any extension of political freedom from the hated

Sasenach UNLESS the utmost freedom were granted Jews. AND HE WON." Cordially addressed to "My dear Governor," the letter probably emanated from Massachusetts Senator David Walsh, himself an Irish Catholic and one of the few Democrats on the committee.

29. Matthew and Hannah Josephson, *Al Smith: Heroe of the Cities* (Boston: Houghton Mifflin, 1969), p. 17.

30. Letter, Julius Frank to Marshall, Oct. 9, 1928, American Jewish Committee Archives. Also *New York Times,* Oct. 6, 1928, p. 21.

31. Letter, Hawes to Wise, Oct. 2, 1928, Wise Papers.

32. Materials and clippings, Massena File, New York State Police, State Campus, Albany, N. Y.

33. London *Times,* Oct. 4, 1928, p. 15.

34. *New York Sun,* Oct. 4, 1928, p. 12.

35. "Hideous Libel Refuted," *Literary Digest,* 99 (Oct. 27, 1928): 34–35.

36. *Massena Observer,* Nov. 8, 1928, p. 7.

37. Interview with Seward Hanmer, Aug. 22, 1971.

38. Interview with Eli Friedman, Aug. 24, 1971.

39. Materials and clippings, Massena File, New York State Police, State Campus, Albany, N. Y.

CHAPTER 13

1. Letter, Major Warner to Marshall, Oct. 4, 1928, American Jewish Committee Archives, New York, General Correspondence File, 1906–1932, Massena Folder.

2. Letter, Marshall to Warner, Oct. 6, 1928, American Jewish Committee Archives.

3. Battle was the principal partner in the law firm of Battle, Miller, Levy, and Van Tine. After the incident, he and Wise exchanged notes, complimenting one another for their efforts. Battle was no silent member of the delegation as he told Wise: "It was in my judgment most desirable that the absurd and atrocious accusation should be promptly and completely controverted and also absolutely and unqualifiedly retracted and withdrawn with an appropriate apology." Letters, Battle to Wise, Oct. 7, 1928, and Wise to Battle, Oct. 8, 1928, Wise Papers, American Historical Society, Massena Folder, Brandeis University.

4. Letter, Marshall to Jake Shulkin, Oct. 6, 1928, American Jewish Committee Archives.

5. Letter, Warner to Governor Smith, Oct. 4, 1928, Smith Papers, Library, New York State Education Department, Albany, N. Y.

6. Massena Memorandum, Oct. 9, 1928, Wise Papers, American Jewish Historical Society.

7. *New York Times,* Oct. 5, 1928, p. 27.

8. *Ibid.*

9. *Ibid.*

10. Letter, Warner to Smith, Oct. 4, 1928, Smith Papers.

11. Letter, Marshall to Warner, Oct. 6, 1928, American Jewish Committee Archives.

12. *Ibid.*

13. Letter, Marshall to Brennglass, Oct. 20, 1928, American Jewish Committee Archives.

14. Letter, Margulies to Wise, Oct. 8, 1928, Wise Papers, American Jewish Historical Society.

15. Clippings, Massena File, New York State Police, State Campus, Albany, N. Y.

16. Shulkin and Brennglass to Marshall, Oct. 4, 1928, American Jewish Committee Archives.

17. Letter, Marshall to Shulkin, Oct. 6, 1928, American Jewish Committee Archives.

18. *Ibid.*

19. *Jewish Daily Bulletin,* Oct. 7, 1928, p. 4.

20. "Massena Blood Libel Scotched," *American Hebrew,* Oct. 12, 1928, pp. 751–768.

21. Letter, Barry O'Neil to Wise, Oct. 6, 1928, Wise Papers, American Jewish Historical Society.

22. Cited in Massena Memorandum, Oct. 9, 1928, Wise Papers, American Jewish Historical Society, and *Jewish Daily Bulletin,* Oct. 7, 1928, pp. 3–4.

23. "Hideous Libel Refuted," *Literary Digest,* Oct. 27, 1928, vol. 99, p. 35.

24. Wire, Julius Frank to Marshall, Oct. 9, 1928, American Jewish Committee Archives.

25. *Ibid.*

26. Letter, Marshall to Frank, Oct. 9, 1928, American Jewish Committee Archives.

27. This is one note that has not survived in the archives.

28. Letter, Marshall to Brennglass, Oct. 20, 1928, American Jewish Commitee Archives.

29. Letter, Hawes to Marshall, Oct. 4, 1928, Wise Papers, American Jewish Historical Society.

Notes

30. *American Jewish Committee: Minutes of the Executive Committee,* vol. 5 (Nov. 17, 1923–Feb. 14, 1932), pp. 1408–1410, American Jewish Committee Archives.

31. Interview with Abe Kauffman, Aug. 20, 1971.

32. No reference is found in Morton Rosenstock, *Louis Marshall, Defender of Jewish Rights* (Detroit: Wayne State University Press, 1965); Charles Reznikoff (ed.), *Louis Marshall: Champion of Liberty* (Philadelphia: Jewish Publication Society of America, 1957); Carl H. Voss, *Stephen S. Wise: Servant of the People* (Philadelphia: Jewish Publication Society of America, 1969); *Challenging Years: The Autobiography of Stephen Wise* (New York: Putnam, 1949); or Justine Wise Polier and James Waterman Wise (eds.), *The Personal Letters of Stephen Wise* (Boston: Beacon, 1956).

33. *Jewish Daily Bulletin,* Oct. 9, 1928, p. 3.

34. Apart from *No Haven for the Oppressed,* other works that discuss the guilt of American Jews during the Holocaust include Arthur Morse, *While Six Million Died* (New York: Random House, 1968); Ben Hecht, *Perfidy* (New York: Julian Messner, 1961); David Wyman, *Paper Walls* (Amherst: University of Massachusetts Press, 1968), And Henry L. Feingold, *The Politics of Rescue* (Rutgers Univ. Press, 1970).

CHAPTER 14

1. *New York Times,* Oct. 7, 1928, p. 31. See also Wise Statement, American Jewish Historical Society, Wise Papers, Massena Folder, Brandeis University.

2. *Massena Observer,* Oct. 18, 1928, p. 1.

3. Interview with Cole Cummins, Aug. 22, 1971.

4. The flyer mentioned specific steps children should take to avoid molesters. Nearby was a circular on a little girl lost in Staunton, Va. Massena police station, Aug. 23, 1971.

5. *History of Massena: The Orphan Town,* Written and published by Eleanor and Nina Dumas (A Massena Bicentennial Production) 1977 p. 142.

6. Interview with Marie Elden-Brown, Aug. 20, 1971.

7. Interview with Jack Jacobs, Aug. 20, 1971.

8. Interview with Seward Hanmer, Aug. 22, 1971.

9. For obvious reasons, I have spared these correspondents the embarrassment of identifying them.

10. One may discover the following statement buried within the

entry "Hugh of Lincoln": "Modern historians, Christian and Jewish, have refuted general charges of such ritual murder by the Jews, and no single case of it has ever been proved." *New Catholic Encyclopedia,* vol. 7 (New York: McGraw-Hill, 1967), p. 192.

11. F. G. Holweck, *A Biographical Dictionary of the Saints (London: Herder, 1924; reprint, 1969), p. 494.*

12. Ibid., p. 919.

13. *Ibid.,* p. 1033.

14. *Ibid.,* p. 1036.

15. *Ibid.,* p. 919.

16. *ZINS Weekly News Bulletin,* Jan. 21, 1972, p. 4.

17. Letter from Jack Jacobs, Sept. 21, 1976.

18. Interviews with Jack Jacobs, Simon Levine, and Dora Cohen, Aug. 20–22, 1971.

19. Interview with American Jewish Congress Executive, Aug. 25, 1971, New York.

INDEX

Index

Hanmer, Seward, *viii,* 77-78, 142, 146, 161, 182
Harrowgate House, 18
Hatfield House, 18
Hawes, W. Gilbert: background, 75-78; interrogation of Shulkin, 82-84; meeting with Jewish leaders, 141-45; pressed for apology, 146-49, 152-55, 158-60; threatened, 161-62; apology, 166-68; mentioned, 63, 81, 109, 163, 165, 169-70, 174-75, 179
Heim, Lt. Edward, 82, 121, 137-38, 140-44, 158, 165, 169, 204
Hill, Joseph Podgorsky, 201
Hitler, Adolph, 98
Hogansburg, 14, 83. *See also* St. Regis Indians
Holiday, Frank, 76
Holiday, Fred, 104
Holocaust, 151, 176-77, 208
Holweck, Rev. F. G., 184
Hoover, Herbert, 3, 6, 147, 179, 190
Host Desecration, 66-67
Hughes, Trooper Ed., 43, 84, 107-8
Husseini, Haj Amin, 53. *See also* Jews, in Palestine
Hutchins, Maud, 124
Hypomania, 194

Indians. *See also* St. Regis Indians
International Jew, The, 94, 98. See also Ford, Henry and *Protocols of Elders of Zion*

Jabotinsky, Vladimir, 177
Jacobs, Jack, *vii,* 62, 72-73, 78, 89, 105, 118, 185, 194, 196, 200
Jewish Holidays. *See* Passover and Yom Kippur
Jewish Labor Committee, 100, 176
Jewish Publication Society of America, 62
Jewish Telegraph Agency, *viii,* 101, 122, 200. *See also* Smolar, Boris
Jews: in Europe, 21, 87-89, 150, 184; in Germany, 176; in Greece, 64-65; in Massena, *passim;* in medicine, 139; in New York City, 90-91; in New York State, 21,

142, 156, 174, 191, 194; in Palestine, 53; in Poland, 52-93, 191; in Russia, 89-90, 92, 150; in Salonika, 64; in slave trade 139; in Spain, 130-31; in U.S., 93-94, 99, 102, 121, 172, 176-77, 205, 208
Joint Distribution Committee, 92, 150
Joly, Maurice, 94
Jones, Dr. Bob, 4

Katz, Jacob, 173
Kauffman, Abe, *vii,* 71, 88, 91, 105, 144, 198, 200
Kauffman, Jesse, 23, 80, 88-91, 105, 107, 109, 120, 143, 162, 164-65, 169, 171, 179, 185
Kirwan, Supt. William, *viii,* 198
Kishinev Pogrom, 89-90, 198
Klein, Mimi Shulkin, *vii,* 55-56, 72-73, 83, 86, 201
Klemens, Mike, 180
Kluger, Richard, *ix*
Know Nothings, 5, 81
Kohler, Kaufmann, 93
Kol Nidre, 47, 87, 119-20, 129-32. *See also Yom Kippur*
Kristallnacht, 176
Krushevan, Paul, 94
Ku Klux Klan: in U.S., 5; in Oklahoma, 6-11; in Massena, 26-29, 38-39; mentioned, 72, 81, 105, 144, 172, 182, 189-90. *See also* Countryman, Roy and Countryman, Willard.

Lehey, Ella, *viii,* 82
Lamedvovnik, 59, 132
Lande, Louis, 165
Lehman, Herbert, 156
Lehman, Irving, 111, 173
Levine, Harry, 73, 201
Levine, Simon, 173
Levy, Aaron, 156
London Times, 159
Louisville, 15, 22, 45
Louisville Courier-Journal, 160
Lusk Bills, 8

Index

Index